NEVE

NEVER ALONE

*Stories of God at work
in family life*

MICHAEL HEWS

Scripture Union

Scripture Union, 207–209 Queensway, Bletchley, MK2 2EB, England.

First published 1997

ISBN 1 85999 098 3

British Library Cataloguing-in-Publication Data
A catalogue record for this book is available from the British Library.

Cover design by Hurlock Design.
Printed and bound in Great Britain by Cox & Wyman Ltd, Reading, Berkshire.

CONTENTS

PREFACE

Real life has never been like those TV ads. The world is not made up of standard nuclear families, with dad, mum, son and daughter smiling together over their bowls of breakfast cereal. It never has been, not even in the days of long ago, and certainly not in Bible times. Families were always assorted, and not just because some had lots of kids and others had none.

However, families today are more assorted than ever. Less than half the households in Britain consist of married couples with dependent children. By the year 2000, one-fifth of all children under sixteen will have experienced the divorce of their parents. More and more people are encountering the complications of relationships after remarriage. More and more people are living on their own. We have seen a rapid rise in the number of single, solo parents.

These are not just statistics. These are people, often hurt and lonely, living in our town, on our street.

It's not all a tale of woe. Life expectancy and living standards have also risen and brought bonuses. Golden weddings are no longer unusual. More children than ever enjoy the friendship and support of active grandparents. And telephones and cars have made it much easier for us to keep in touch with scattered relatives.

In this book, people with a varied assortment of family histories and family experiences tell their own stories. We have felt it wise to change some of their names, but I can assure you that they are all real people! I have met them and interviewed them, and I have found myself excited and often very moved as I listened to what they had to say.

I have been encouraged, too, because these stories show God at work in families of all kinds. The good news of Jesus is for everyone, and in our churches we need to welcome everyone with his love. Then, together, we can listen to God who, through the scriptures and the illumination of his Spirit, will tell us how we are to live and how we need to change.

Jesus never said life would be easy, even for the most devoted of his followers, and this book bears that out. He also made it clear that sometimes members of the same family would be at loggerheads because they disagreed about him (Matt 10:35–39). There are examples in this book of converts to Christ who for years had to endure fierce opposition from within their own families.

But they, and all of us who have likewise come to faith, are one in Christ Jesus, whatever our family histories. We belong to the biggest and best family in all the world, the family of Christian believers. In such a family and with such a Father, how can we ever be alone?

Michael Hews

Chapter 1

THE CHILDHOOD SHE HAS
NEVER FORGOTTEN

Twenty-year-old Caroline had fallen behind with her rent. Her husband had left her – and left her to pay the bills – and she had a two-year-old daughter, Emma.

Barry had had a chequered career. He had been a milkman, a self-employed tree-feller and a civil servant in two government departments. He was now thirty-nine and working as an area arrears officer for the local city council. Caroline was one of the defaulters he had to call on regularly. She used to make him a cup of tea. Barry noticed all the kids playing in her garden.

Caroline has loads of memories of her childhood, and they are mostly bad. 'I remember being beaten by my stepfather, being accused of things I hadn't done and thrown down the stairs. I grew up with my stepfather calling me "ugly". He would say nearly every day that nobody loved me, and that if I'd been any good my real father wouldn't have left before I was born. He kept saying that my father always knew what I'd be like.'

When she was about eight, her older brother and sister left to stay with her dad. 'This was more ammunition for my stepfather – obviously my dad didn't want *me*.'

'Times when I just didn't want to live'

The physical and emotional bruising took their toll. 'I had a lot of problems because of the way my stepfather treated me. I wanted to cry out. I wanted someone to believe me. So many times I had "hidden" bruises. There were times when I just didn't want to live.

'I often had to look after my two younger brothers. They were lovely. My youngest brother, Colin, saved my life once, though he didn't know it...'

One evening, after she had put her two young brothers to bed, Caroline got out a bottle of pills and started taking them one by one. 'I decided I'd had enough, I wanted to put an end to it. I thought that, without me, life would be better for all the family.'

She isn't sure how many pills she got through before she heard Colin start to whimper. He tended to have tantrums all the neighbours could hear! 'I knew I would have to do something drastic, so I made myself sick to get rid of the pills. Then, when I had tended to Colin, I sat down to think about what I'd done. I prayed I would never feel like that again.'

Over the next few days she was quite ill. Her mother thought it was a bout of flu. Caroline never told her the truth.

There were two places where Caroline could escape from the traumas of home. One was her local parish church. 'I went to church a lot. I loved it.' She has happy memories of ice-skating with the youth group and of overnight trips away.

The other place of escape was the top of the long garden. 'I knew my stepfather couldn't touch me there. We had a swing which I felt was my special place to talk to God. I would swing to my heart's content, telling God all my problems and singing at the top of my voice. I knew God would know how I was feeling.

'But I never completely escaped. There would always come a time when I had to go back to the house and to my stepfather.'

Growing up

Once during her childhood Caroline spent a few days with foster-parents. 'To leave your own parent is a very traumatic experience. No matter how nice your foster-parents are, they can never take the place of your natural parents. But simple things, like where you're going to sleep, can make a big difference to how you settle down. And when I not only heard an ice-cream van but was given the money to buy an ice-cream, I thought I was in heaven.'

As a teenager she became a bit of a rebel. 'I never hurt anybody but I was into smoking and under-age drinking. For a while I trained as a nurse. Around this time my mother divorced my stepfather. Then I got pregnant with Emma.'

She married Emma's father, but even as she was walking down the aisle she knew it was a big mistake. Six months later her husband left her. So began the rent arrears that Barry had to collect.

Barry had been born in Lichfield during the war. He came from a stable family but, like Caroline, he too began to kick over the traces as a teenager.

'I had a number of girlfriends and eventually, at twenty-three, I got married – we *had* to get married. My wife came from a Methodist background and I used to go along to church just to please her and her parents. We had four kids in four and a half years.

'At work I was promoted to a job in the north-west of England. But the moment we were on the train to go north, I had a sinking feeling – I knew I had made a mistake.' Barry had a major breakdown and his employers moved the family back to their home area, on compassionate grounds. Like Caroline, though in different circumstances, Barry took an overdose.

'I was very depressed. I took a hundred sleeping tablets and forty anti-depressants, and ended up, much to my horror, in a psychiatric hospital. Three days of my life I just can't remember. Now, when I meet people suffering from depression, I never make judgements – I've been there.'

Barry recovered. He left his job at the Ministry of Defence on the grounds of conscience, and became a Jehovah's Witness. These were turbulent years in his life. Like Caroline, he experienced the pain of marital break-down: his first marriage failed and, after just a couple of years, so did his second. Meanwhile, he had two spells working for the Department of Social Security, and was briefly a milkman and a tree-feller before becoming an area arrears office for his local housing authority.

A pastor, who knew Barry had problems, asked if he could come and see him. They went for a walk together, up a hill, and when they reached the top the pastor asked, 'Would you like me to pray for you?' Barry said yes, and the pastor prayed for him there and then, with people passing by. Barry was impressed!

A big surprise

Barry confesses that as a boy he went to Sunday School just to play about. His memories of church were 'a dark building where people dressed in black, nobody smiled and you were bored out of your mind'. So he had a big surprise when, one Sunday morning, he went with two friends to a church that met in a school. 'There were four hundred people there and they all looked happy.'

Having been a Marxist and a Trade Union spokesman, Barry was slightly sceptical. However, he couldn't help but be impressed by the spontaneity of the worship. 'After three hours, it seemed as if I'd been there for ten minutes.'

At the end the preacher said, 'There's a man here whom God wants to forgive his sins.' Barry realised that man was himself. 'I felt twenty feet tall and really cleansed. I had a heap of sins. I was living alone then, and later that day I was washing up in my flat when it hit me what Jesus had done for me. I just broke down and cried. I cried with joy.'

The next Sunday, Barry had the experience of being filled with the Spirit. In the weeks that followed, his pastor was amazed at the speed of his spiritual growth. But Barry had the advantage of being no stranger to the Bible. For two years he had been an ardent, door-knocking Jehovah's Witness. Although he had picked up many wrong interpretations he needed to unlearn, he had acquired a thorough knowledge of the Bible. Now, he says, 'I began *really* to look into scripture.'

When he was converted, he made an appointment to see his doctor whom he knew was a Christian. That same doctor had treated him when he had taken the drug overdose. 'I went into his surgery and he asked me what was wrong. I said, "There's nothing wrong. I've come to tell you I've become a Christian!" The joy that came into that man's face!'

'Lord, you must be joking...'

As a new convert Barry was advised, 'You've had problems with women. You've had two broken marriages. Stay single and serve the Lord.'

It sounded very good advice. But rent arrears still have to be collected, even at Easter, and when he called on Caroline she gave him an Easter card and her two-year-old daughter gave him a chocolate egg. As he drove away from her house that day, Barry said, 'Lord, you must be joking! There's an eighteen-year age-gap between us!'

However, he began to share his faith with Caroline and to take her out. He invited her to church and she too came to faith in Christ.

'A long time to relate to God as Father'

Her conversion wasn't as dramatic as Barry's, but proved equally real. 'It was as if the Lord was quietly reaching down. All through my childhood I'd been told I wasn't loved. Now I realised there was someone who did love me. But I'd had such a bad experience of my human father, it took me a long time to relate to God as Father.'

Caroline and Barry were married. Some Christians were supportive, others were not. Barry feels strongly that churches today need to be ready to cope with newcomers who have been divorced once or maybe twice before they came to faith in Christ. 'The Lord hates divorce, *I* hate divorce. But I know the Lord has forgiven not just some of my sins, but *all* my sins.'

Caroline's mother predicted their relationship wouldn't last more than three months. That was fifteen years ago. They now have two teenage daughters of their own, but they regard Barry's son and three daughters by his first marriage and Caroline's daughter, Emma, (all of whom have now left home) as their own children too.

'The Lord has brought us through'

The last fifteen years have not been entirely a bed of roses. But, Barry says, 'the Lord has brought us through. When Caroline had cancer, the Lord healed her. When I was unemployed, it was Christmas and we had nothing in the house, there was a knock on the door – standing there were two Christian friends bringing us a box of goodies.

'When our daughter Sharlene was born, it was eight minutes before she began to breathe. There was pandemonium in the delivery room as the medical team swung into action. When at last she let out a little whimper, I shouted, "Hallelujah!" One of the doctors came up to me and said, "Are you a Christian? So am I!"

'We have been blessed more than abundantly when we were in dire situations and had to rely on the Lord.'

But Caroline has never forgotten her own childhood. 'When I was a child, there was nobody there when I needed help.' This is why, three years ago, Caroline and Barry began fostering.

They have seen dramatic changes in some of their foster-children in the course of a few months; others have not been easy. 'Some we feel we have failed, even though social services say we haven't. As foster-parents you can find yourself in a no-win situation.

'We always make it clear that our foster-children will be treated no differently from our own children, and they have the same discipline.'

'We've learnt from our mistakes'

'Caroline definitely has a special gift with children,' says Barry. But what most foster-children lack is a father-figure. 'Social services have given me some quite good reports, and we have been commended many a time. But we have learnt from our mistakes.'

'We've got a real challenge coming up,' says Caroline. 'We're taking on a five-year-old boy who has never had any stable relationships. He can't speak properly and he's said to be very violent. I'm looking forward to that...'

'Fostering is a high-stress job,' says Barry, 'but we always have the Lord to lean on. We're always open with social services and tell them we'll be taking our foster-children with us to church. We know children have benefited from that. Seeds are sown. We pray together as a family, and we have communion together as a family, at home during Sunday lunch-time.'

'I know what they're going through'

On the whole, their own daughters have coped very well with the situation. 'They have a lot to put up with. They've had clothes stolen, they've been threatened with a knife, and they lose their privacy. There was one girl they didn't particularly like. We were glad to see her go too.

'With one exception, we have taken our two daughters with us on all the courses run by social services for foster-parents. After all, they're carers, too. The one exception was the course on coping with sexual abuse. Social services said no to their going to that, probably because of what other foster-parents might think.'

Caroline feels she is a better foster-mother because of what she herself went through in her own childhood. 'I'm more sympathetic to the children. I've been there. I can feel for them because I know what it's like. I know they're not just being naughty. They're crying out for help.'

Extra love

Their church has also taken extra special care to welcome the children. 'They try to give extra love. It's a very welcoming church. The worship is lively, and the people obviously enjoy coming. It's a church for all ages.'

Caroline is not only a wife, mother and foster-mother. She is a child-minder, too. 'When our daughters had whooping cough, I gave up my job in a school – I used to help with the children with special needs. However, I felt that as a mother my job was with the children at home, so I applied to be a child-minder.

'Nearly all the children I've minded are from Christian families and have come by personal recommendation. It's very difficult to find a Christian child-minder. As a Christian, I would want a Christian to mind my own children. I would want to make sure they were safe spiritually.

'Where I've had children with special needs through the social services, I've sometimes had to take on the parents as well. I've had to help them know how to say no to their children and how to discipline them without lashing out.'

Their neighbours don't want them to move

Barry now works for a firm of funeral directors. He and

Caroline and their family live in a three-bedroom ex-council house. They bought it for a very reasonable price. It's on a local authority estate which hasn't always enjoyed the best of reputations.

'The neighbours know we are believers. We've managed to put Bibles into nearly every house in our immediate neighbourhood, and nearly all the children in this square have been to Sunday School. If neighbours swear and we're about, they apologise. In the early days, we had a good deal of mocking, but that's changed and recently two lads cleaned the church minibus for us.'

When I visited Barry and Caroline, their house was on the market. But their neighbours didn't want them to go! 'If anybody comes to buy the house, they say they're going to turn on loud music so as to put them off. They're going to chain themselves to the gate and put a wheel clamp on our car so that we can't move.'

Meanwhile, Barry and Caroline are giving their extended family the love Caroline never knew as a child. Barry remembers how, fifteen years ago, he noticed all the children playing in Caroline's garden. Smiling, he says, 'The difference now is that they're playing in mine.'

Chapter 2

'GOD'S FAMILY IS MY FAMILY'

Kal's parents came to Birmingham from India in the 1960s. Her dad worked for a leading industrial company until he was made redundant eight or nine years ago. Her mum does sewing at home for a local factory and gets a very low wage. Kal is one of seven children: she has three older sisters, and one older and two younger brothers.

'I grew up with incense and idols and images in the house. Every now and then Mum and Dad would go off to the temple to celebrate one of the gurus' birthdays. As I grew older, Mum became really involved. She went to the temple every Tuesday night, and on Sundays too.'

It was when she went to secondary school that Kal first saw very clearly the difference between her own upbringing and nearly everyone else's. 'I wore the uniform, but with trousers. All the other girls wore skirts. Even some of the Asian girls wore skirts – their parents were more liberal.'

'I just wanted not to be different'

'My hair was long and I wore it in two plaits. I never really wanted to have my hair cut or to wear make-up. I just wanted not to be different. I stuck out like a sore thumb.'

There were other differences too. 'I had to go straight home from school. The other girls could go to one another's houses, but I couldn't. They could stop over at night, but I couldn't. My friends weren't really allowed to come round and see me. If the phone went and it was for me, I'd have an anxiety attack because I knew Dad would have something to say. My mum would panic too, because she knew he'd go barmy.

'It was as if I had to play two separate roles. At school I was everybody's friend, and at home I was my parents' daughter.

'What was so unfair is that my brothers weren't restricted in the same way. In the culture I grew up in, daughters are seen as a burden. They have to be married off, there's the dowry and all the gold you have to provide. Whereas with sons it's the opposite – they bring money into the family, so they're more honoured.

'You could always see the differences between the sons and the daughters in our family. When Mum came back from shopping, she would bring two chocolate bars for my brothers and just penny sweets for us. These little things spoke so loudly. They built up such feelings of rejection.

'I grew up with Dad saying to me, "If you die, I'll bury you in the garden and I'll save about £5,000 on your wedding." *And he wasn't joking.* He meant it. Growing up, I knew I was a burden. It made me feel terrible. It still does. If I stand back and look at it objectively, I can understand this attitude because of the expense. But if I personalise it, it hurts.

'You knew you weren't as good as the boys, and you wanted to be. So I would always try my hardest to please Mum and Dad. I spent hours working at the sewing machine. I'd get up early in the morning and keep sewing till late at night, so that we could sell clothes to the factory Mum worked for, and have some extra money coming into the house. I'd do all the cooking and all the cleaning. I'd do everything I could to get my parents to accept me and value me.

'Dad would tell me that because of the extra work he'd

put aside so many extra pounds or ounces in gold for when I got married. But I thought, *I don't really care for gold or clothes. I only want you to accept me and love me because I'm me.*

'When I came home from school, I'd have to wash the breakfast dishes and the dinner-time dishes, and then cook everybody's tea. They would eat first and I would have to wait until they had finished.'

'School was an escape'

'School work was hard, but school for me was an escape from my home situation. People intrigued me at school. I used to watch various characters and think, *Why do you do that?* I made a friend called Linda, who I'm still in touch with. She used to read murder mysteries and she got me hooked on them.

'In third year a new girl called Sue arrived. Everybody in the class respected her. I used to watch her and think, *What's the big deal about Sue? What's the difference between her and me? Why do they treat her differently?* I used to be really loud at school, simply because I wanted to be heard and wasn't heard at home.

'We were divided up into ability groups, and Sue ended up in all the same classes as Linda and me. She started talking to us about being a Christian and how Jesus healed. She told us about this woman – she must have had eczema of some sort. Then somebody prayed for her. Sue said that by the next day her skin was as smooth as a baby's bottom.

'I used to call Sue a dreamer because I couldn't conceive in my head how what she said could possibly happen. I knew Jesus had come down to earth because I'd watched a film about him on TV. I knew he'd died but I couldn't get into my head that he was still very much alive and active.

'The amazing thing is that our whole family used to sit and watch films about Jesus. I remember my dad crying. He

was so angry they had killed an innocent man. He would
swear something chronic.'

'She had brought something just for me'

'One Friday Sue brought two New Testaments and gave
them to Linda and me. It wasn't the fact that it was a New
Testament that touched me: it was that she had brought
something just for me. All I usually had were hand-me-
downs. If I ever needed something new, I was made to feel
guilty that Mum and Dad had to spend so much money on
me.

'Off I trundled home with my New Testament. I had
already read the Gospels – that was when I was about nine.
My half-brother had been given a big, blue King James
Bible by the Gideons. I remember reading Matthew and
thinking, *Wow!* At the time I didn't know I had to ask Jesus
to come and live in my heart. But I tried desperately hard to
be good by my own efforts. My brothers and sisters and I
used to call each other terrible names, and I tried not to
retaliate. That lasted about a month!'

So, when Kal started to read the New Testament Sue had
given her, she didn't turn to the Gospels but to the book of
Revelation. 'It must have been by the goodness of God that
I knew all the things described in it were going to happen. I
was terrified. I knew I wasn't going to get to heaven
because my life was in a state. I remember sitting there
reading, with the sun shining into the lounge, thinking, *I've
got to do something. I'm going to become a Christian.*

'Mum was in the loo at the time – ours is an outside toilet, like a little shed in the garden. So off I trundled thinking, *I'm going to do something right for the first time in my
life.* I banged on the loo door and said, "Mum, can I become
a Christian?"

'Well, she went mad! She started cursing and threaten-
ing. I couldn't understand why because I wanted to do

something good! So I panicked and ran back into the house. I thought, *If she gets hold of me, I've had it!* I hurried upstairs and tried to hide as flat as I could under the duvet.'

'I knew I was in serious trouble'

'Mum stamped up the stairs, found me and dragged me down to the front room. Dad was out at the pub – he was an alcoholic by this stage – but Mum called in all my brothers and sisters. I was sobbing. I just couldn't understand what was going on. All I knew was that I was in serious trouble because of this Christianity thing. Mum told my brothers and sisters what I wanted to do, and they stood there and mocked me.

'Mum thought I wanted to forsake being an Indian and become a white person – that was her real fear. But one of my brothers, with whom I had a good relationship, said, "If that's what she wants to do, let her do it." Mum totally humiliated him, and he backed off. Then they all left me. But in my heart I knew I had stumbled across something and I couldn't let it go.

'I knew Mum wouldn't tell Dad because she was afraid he might kill me. So I just went to my room and had a good cry and thought, *What am I going to do?* I was leading a double life anyway. But somewhere in my heart the decision had been made, and I knew it was impossible to turn back.

'I went to school on the Monday, found Sue and said, "I want to become a Christian." And Sue cried. I'd given her such a hard time before, because I couldn't understand what she was on about. She cried, and she cried, and she cried. And I couldn't think what she was crying for, because Sue isn't a person who cries! But she was crying because she thought there was no hope for me. She was overwhelmed by it all.'

Macbeth and an evangelist

'The next step was to get me to a church, and we agonised over this for hours. Eventually we decided – and I know now that it was very wrong – that I would tell Mum we were going to see *Macbeth* after school. We got a lift to a friend's house, had tea there, and then Sue, Linda and I went off to a local Pentecostal church. An evangelist was conducting a series of weekday evening meetings there.

'I remember sitting in the car outside this church, knowing that if I went inside I would never be the same again. I had such a struggle going on inside, it was as if the old me was fighting to hold on. I said to Sue, "I'm not going in." She said, "Well, you can get the bus home, because I *am* going in." I'm glad now she said that because I didn't know where the bus was to go home, did I? I went in because I was annoyed with Sue!

'It was like walking into another world. Our household isn't affectionate. No one ever gives anyone a hug or a kiss. So, walking into a place where people were loving one another and hugging one another, I thought, *What is this? I don't understand it, but I like it!*'

'I didn't know what a sinner was'

'I couldn't tell you what the evangelist preached on, but the atmosphere was amazing. Then they did the altar call and up we trundled, Linda and I, with Sue. We went round to the back of the church and a friend of ours counselled us. She asked if we wanted to become Christians and we nodded. She asked if we knew we were sinners. Well, I didn't know what a sinner was, and I'm sitting there watching Linda and if she nods, then I'm going to nod. Words like "sinner" and "asking forgiveness for sin" are a whole different language, aren't they? So we prayed this prayer. We didn't know what it meant, but we prayed it. Then we left, with everyone saying "Well done" to Sue because she had brought Linda and me along.

'Sue tried to explain my home situation to the evangelist and he basically told us not to do anything drastic.

'The worse thing about coming home was that I had experienced something awesome which I wanted to share with my family and I couldn't. I couldn't tell them what had happened to me and, at the same time, I couldn't contain it.

'Anyway, we went to see "Macbeth" again the next night! The evangelist did another altar call, this time for people who wanted prayer for healing. I thought, *That doesn't apply to me*, but the next thing I knew, I was going to the front of the church. I took Linda with me. They had this line, with people standing behind those waiting for prayer. The preacher moved down the line, praying for people, and he got to Linda before he got to me. He must have prayed for her to be filled with the Holy Spirit because the next thing is, Linda's on the floor! So I think, *What is going on?*'

Kal felt her fear ebb away and being replaced by anticipation. When the preacher asked her what she wanted, she said, 'Some of what she's got!'

'I didn't know any better. So he explained things and prayed for me, and I had the most real encounter I've ever had with God. I don't think I'd be here today if it hadn't happened. I couldn't have made it through all that followed.'

'God was as real as real could be'

'There was this brilliant, white light and I knew without a shadow of a doubt that this God was real, as real as real could be.

'That night it was even worse coming home and trying to be myself. I just couldn't stop smiling. In bed I was giggling all night long because I'd got something and it was real and it was mine. But I couldn't share it.

'However, though Mum and Dad didn't know I was a Christian, everything at home became absolutely dreadful. The name-calling got worse. I couldn't understand it – how

I'd found something so real and yet everything at home was turning upside down.

'I went into school feeling upset and angry. I kept asking, "What is going on?" We didn't know about spiritual warfare then. I remember walking down the road with Sue, all my anger and hurt coming out: "Why is this happening to me now I've become a Christian? Why, why, why?!" Sue couldn't answer because she didn't know how to.

'God must have reassured me deep down, because later I went to Sue and told her, "I'm going to stick with this. There isn't anything else for me." And we had a good old cry together.

'We would sit in biology together and try to work out how to alleviate my home situation. We actually planned for me to leave home after my fifth year at school and go to Wales. But one weekend we prayed about this and we felt it wouldn't be right. We agonised over what to do again and again.

'Friends from Sue's church would write and ask me to stay with them for the weekend. This would distress me, because I felt they didn't understand why I couldn't go. And if Christians couldn't understand, then what *was* I going to do?'

Marriage – or India?

'My friend John and his wife were one of the couples who invited me to visit so that they could love me and help me. I wrote back saying that I recognised now what a family in God was. Sue and Linda were my family because they loved me. From what I could see, my family at home didn't. I also said in this letter that I was a Christian and I was looking to leave home.

'This letter was in my school bag and, of course, my sister used to go through all my things. She found it and took it to my mum. When I got home, what a reception! I was so frightened. Mum threatened to take me out of school. She threatened me with marriage. She threatened to send me away to India. And my sisters were so hateful. They let me know they thought I was scum.

'But I praise God that at this point Mum said, "You can read your Bible if you want to, you can believe what you believe if you want to. But if you dare set foot outside this house to go to church, if you dare tell anyone in this family you are a Christian, you're as good as dead!"

'Mum came up to school. She wanted me away from the class, away from Linda, away from Sue. So all our teachers got involved. Linda, Sue and I were so distressed that our grades dropped from As to Cs.

'During the long summer break, Linda would come to the house and Sue would wait just round the corner. But my sister would slam the door in Linda's face, and I'd have to sneak out later. Linda and Sue were my support throughout that time. There wasn't anybody else. I felt so alone, I couldn't see any way out, so I tried to take an overdose. I didn't take enough pills because I was afraid of the pain, and nothing much happened. But I was really down, really troubled.

'This is where both my nieces come into the story. I spent quite a lot of time with them and we had a really good relationship. I talked to them about becoming a Christian, I just witnessed and witnessed and witnessed – and one of them gave her life to the Lord. She and I spent time together, listening to Christian music tapes, talking and sharing how we felt about things. Eventually my other niece gave her life to the Lord as well.

'So that made three of us. Every weekend we would see one another, sometimes during the week as well. We prayed for one another and read the Bible together. We didn't always understand what we were reading, but we would have a good old read anyway!

'The teachers at school had told Mum there was no way they could separate Sue and Linda and me. But they were giving Sue a hard time, asking her what right she had to change somebody else's faith and cause all these upsets. In fact, Mum said it was OK for Sue to come to our house, so Sue would go to church on a Sunday, then come round and teach me whatever she had learned. If we heard Mum come upstairs, then – whoosh! – Bibles would go under the bed and school books would come out. But when we were reading and praying together, a tremendous peace would descend on the room. It was awesome. God was so real.'

No turning back

'I remember a time when the gas bills were too high and I didn't dare put the heater on. I'd done my usual Saturday routine of cleaning the house from top to bottom, and I lay down on my bed and dozed off. But I woke up feeling warm, as if God had put a blanket over me. It was amazing things like that which convinced me God is real. I knew there was no turning back.

'There were dry times in our lives when my nieces and I would say to each other, "Do you feel as if you're in a rowing boat going round and round in circles and getting nowhere?" Then we would repent and look for encouragement in the Bible, and get back with God and help one another through.'

By the back entrance

Kal was still at school when she noticed a Christian bookshop in the main road near where she lived. At first she would go in through the front entrance to buy books. *Run, Baby, Run* by Nicky Cruz was the first Christian book she read. However, she knew she might be seen going into the bookshop. So, when the situation at home became more traumatic, she went in through the back way.

'There were times when all I would do in the bookshop was cry, and Trevor and Tig (Scripture Union staff member Margaret Owen) would cry with me. There were many times like that.'

Kal left school and went to help in a children's nursery. 'I did a lot of voluntary work, just to get out of the house. Then I decided to go to college to qualify as a social worker, so that I could support myself if I left home. Off I trundled to Coventry in the hope that it was far enough away for my parents to agree to let me stay there. But they still wanted me to live at home. It was stressful. I'd come home and have to do the cleaning *and* my homework. I just don't know how I passed my first-year exams. It was by the grace of God.'

'Put on your best suit and your high heels'

'One Saturday morning I woke up to find that Mum, Dad and everyone else were out. This was abnormal, and in my heart I knew something wasn't right. I sat there with a cup of tea, still in my nightie, wondering what on earth was going on.

'I panicked, managed to pray a quick prayer, and had gone back to my bedroom when everybody came in – my sister-in-law and half-brother, and Mum and Dad. My sister-in-law came straight upstairs to me, which was unusual. She and I have never got on. She said, "Put on your best suit." I said, "Put on my best suit – for what?" She told me we were going to see a man – for me.

'The shock that hit my body. Everything went numb, and after the numbness I shook from head to foot. Every muscle, every fibre in my body was shaking. I have never experienced anything like it before or since. I couldn't get a grip on my body because I just couldn't believe what she had just said to me. She was really happy: for her it was a grand occasion. I was trying hard not to cry hysterically.

'I got out my best suit and ironed it, and did my hair. Dad shouted up the stairs, "Put on your high heels" – apparently this man, whoever he might be, was very tall. So there I was, having had no breakfast and shaking like a leaf, coming down the stairs in my high heels and thinking, *What am I going to do?*'

'How am I going to get out of this?'

'They were all downstairs. Mum smiled at me approvingly. I gathered this man was going to be at my sister-in-law's house, which was good because my nieces would be there. We drove over. My mind was racing: *How am I going to get out of this? How?*

'As soon as I reached the house, I ran up the stairs and into the arms of my nieces. They were panic-stricken. I just held onto them and sobbed. Mum and Dad and the others were shouting to me to come down the stairs. I pulled myself together and said to my nieces, "Pray! Whatever you do, pray!"

'The men were in the front room and the women were in the lounge. After a bit, the others went out and left me on my own. Then in walked this man. I'll never forget it. He was divorced, he was terribly obese and he wasn't very nice at all.

'I don't know how I managed not to walk out of that room. All the anger I felt was suddenly unleashed on this man. He didn't know what hit him! I told him, "I'm a Christian and I'm not marrying anyone who's not!"

'He went and told everyone in the front room what I'd said. You can imagine what happened. There was an absolute riot! All I could think was, *Thank you, Jesus. I've got out of it.*

'Everybody piled back into the room, cursing at me because I'd humiliated them all. I thought the best thing to do was just to take it and say nothing. They got really nasty about my physical appearance, saying, "Who's going to want to marry you anyway?"

'I was desperate to get in touch with Sue to ask her to pray, but by this time she was studying in Leicester. So I was constantly in that Christian bookshop.

'At home my brothers were calling me all sorts of terrible things. Mum would cook but not serve me. Dad would just sit and cry. I knew he had been hurt and I was responsible. It really tormented me.

'I told Mum I wasn't going to get married, I was a Christian and I wasn't going to see anybody else. But my sister, who was three or four months pregnant at the time, tried to blackmail me into seeing some more men. She said, "If you won't get married, I'm going to kill my baby." And I knew she was the kind of person who would do it.

'In the end I gave in. The despair! I felt so lost. I felt I'd let myself down, I'd let God down, and I'd let my nieces down. If I had been strong in this area and said no, then there would have been hope for them. But I just couldn't handle the trauma and the emotional blackmail.

'My nieces were angry with me. All I could say to them was "If I have to get married, I'll get a divorce and find a place and send for you." That was our plan of action. It seemed the only way.

'I was forced into a routine. Every weekend there was someone to see, and out would come the best suit and the high heels. I came to hate that suit. If I could have burnt it, I would have done. If I could have thrown those high heels at someone, I would have thrown them.

'Call it manipulation, but you learned what to say. You learned to get information out of him. If he didn't want to get married, you were all right: you wouldn't get the stick, he would.

'My nieces and I used to list all the men I'd seen, give them nicknames and then have a laugh. It was our way of coping. There were forty-nine men on the list. I went through the same routine forty-nine times.'

'She asked me to renounce my Christianity'

'I remember my sister coming upstairs – the same one who had threatened to kill her baby – and asking me to renounce my Christianity for the sake of Mum and Dad and so that I'd find someone to marry me. She said I could become a Christian again after I'd got married. I lost control and screamed at her, "It's one thing for you to get me to see all these men, but it's quite another to ask me to give up the very thing I live for!" I was in a violent rage thinking, *What are you going to ask me to do next?* I went into the next room where my nieces were. They saw then that being a Christian wasn't a part-time thing for me – it was my life. No one could take it from me.

'However, I did reach a compromise with Mum and Dad that I wouldn't tell anyone I was a Christian. So I had to find another way round the problem.

'The emotional blackmail continued, and so did the humiliation, every time I turned somebody down. The amazing thing was that my sister *did* miscarry the child she had threatened to kill. She carried him for seven months and then she lost him. Whether she was reaping what she had sown, I wouldn't want to say. But I knew in my heart that she hadn't lost the child because of me. I consoled her as best I could. We all did, because it was a terrible thing.'

'I knew I couldn't get out of this one'

'By the summer holidays, Mum had had enough. Dad was always crying, but his hurt would turn to anger and he would rage at me. He hit me a couple of times, and you knew when Dad hit you because you ended up on the other side of the room.

'Then Mum found this man for me, and it turned out he

was someone I knew! We had been to school together and I had liked him then. I thought, *This is it. I can't get out of this one.*

'Despair overwhelmed me. I lay on my bed and said, "I've got three options, God. Get married and then get divorced. Commit suicide" – and this was a serious option – "I could do myself in and leave what I've saved (about £3000) to my nieces so they can run away from home. Or leave home myself." '

Kal was fearful that if she left, her mum and dad would see God as the one who takes daughters away, and would never ever come to him. 'I was in so much torment. I went over to my nieces and told them I was going to do myself in and leave them my money. They hugged me and said, "We're not worth it! We're not worth you doing yourself in!" '

'Leaving all to follow Christ'

'I didn't see why I should I get married and then divorced. So in my heart I knew leaving home was the only way out. I just didn't want to face it. But every scripture I turned to seemed to be about being willing to forsake father and mother and leave all to follow Christ. I struggled and struggled, and eventually I said to God, "If that's the way forward, I'll do it." It was only then that I had peace in my heart. I connected that peace with God and thought, *That's it!*

Kal was now twenty-one. She decided that during the ten-week break from the polytechnic, she would do a typing course because she couldn't bear to be at home. 'I shared my plan to leave home with Sue and she said she would pray for me. I also told Tig, who at first tried to dissuade me, but eventually she agreed I should leave.'

Smuggling clothes out in a typewriter case

'The next thing was to get my clothes out of the house. I bought myself a typewriter, and I would leave the typewriter at the place where I did my course and carry just the case home. Then I crammed as many clothes as I could into the empty case and took it to a friend's house. I bought myself some more clothes and stored them there. And I'd leave home wearing two pairs of trousers or two jumpers and then take one set off at my friend's house. That's how we did it.

'We also needed to find a place for me to go. We prayed and prayed all through the summer, but we couldn't find anywhere that wasn't too close to home. In my heart I knew it was going to work out somehow. I said to God, "If you don't find a place for me until the weekend before I leave home, then so be it." And that's how it was. We found a place in a Christian community in the West Country, and Tig and Scilla (who was then her volunteer assistant) were to drive me down there.

'The amazing thing was that all my family turned up at our house the weekend before I was to go. I hadn't told anyone I was leaving, not even my nieces because I knew how much stress they'd be under if I did.'

'I kept looking over my shoulder'

'My last day at home was 2 October. My mum never used to come into my bedroom in the morning, but that day she came in twice. My heart was thumping because I knew she only had to grab hold of me to find out I was wearing two jumpers and two pairs of jeans.

'It was the first official day back at the polytechnic. I got as far as the front door with two bags containing all my college folders, when suddenly Dad called me back. I started shaking. He said, "You've forgotten your dinner money." So I took my dinner money!

'It was a fifteen-minute walk to my friend's house, but it felt like an eternity. I kept looking over my shoulder to see if anyone was following me. When I finally got there, I took off my second jumper and second pair of jeans, and waited for Tig and Scilla. I don't think the reality of the situation had hit me at all. We piled everything into the car and I lay down on the back seat until we were out of Birmingham.

'Even when we got to the West Country, my mind kept saying, "You can still go back. It'll just be as if you've come home from the poly a bit late!" When we arrived, and got out of the car, and unpacked all my stuff, and were walking round the building, this was still going on in my mind. After Tig and Scilla drove away, it was terrible! That's when I knew there was no turning back. I knew I'd done it.'

A letter home

'I had phoned the local police station to tell them I hadn't been kidnapped or raped – I was alive and well and had left home. I explained why I didn't want to ring up my parents and tell them this. The police were very helpful and agreed to phone my mum and dad for me, and they did.' Kal also wrote a letter to her parents, not giving them any address, which Tig posted back in the Birmingham area so that it wouldn't have a tell-tale postmark.

The family reaction

'All my brothers went driving around looking for me. They went as far as Nottingham. They went all round Leicester and Coventry. They went to the head of my department at the poly. I'd been to see him myself before I left, and had asked him to put my course on hold for a year. He was really good about it. I left an address where he could contact me. When my family turned up at the polytechnic, he told them he knew where I was but because of confidentiality he wasn't prepared to tell them. They could give him letters and he would forward the letters on to me.

'Usually these letters were "Come home and we'll do anything for you" emotional stuff. My parents didn't tell people the reason I'd disappeared. They simply said I'd gone away to study, and in the meantime they had the police in Coventry looking for me as a missing person. They knew that the police in Birmingham wouldn't.

'A policewoman in Coventry who was involved in the hunt actually traced me, but my nieces managed to explain to her what had happened. When she spoke to me over the phone and I told her why I had left home, she said she had suspected as much and that if I ever needed her, she would be there. I thought, *That's brilliant!*

'My parents never stopped looking for me and eventually they got a clue through my doctor. Just before Christmas, during our Christmas Eve party, I had a phone call from a friend who said, "They know where you are!" Of course I panicked. But in fact all my parents knew was that my medical records had been transferred to the West Country.

'Meanwhile, leaders of the Christian community were encouraging me to get back in touch with my family. But here was the first place I'd ever been where I could walk down the road without fear, without the need to keep looking over my shoulder.'

'Never had an Asian there before'

'The difficulty was, no one in the community had come across a situation like mine. In fact, they had never had an Asian there before. I would have to explain my whole story from the beginning before they could begin to understand and before I could begin to express how I felt. I wasn't really given the time do that, so I just suppressed it all and got on with my life. Everyone I knew was so far away. The people in the community did their best to be friendly, but nobody took me under their wing. Some would avoid me because they just didn't understand. The first week I was there, I would do the chores I was given and then just go back to my room and sit.

'The girls on the house-team were really good. I was scrubbing carpets with one who wanted to know about me. Well, you regurgitate your story and you don't realise how horrific other people find it. You think it's normal, it's just what happened. But this girl stopped scrubbing and dissolved into floods of tears. I couldn't understand why she was crying. We sat there on the floor, having a good weep and a good hug.

'The only way I could express myself was through writing poems. And I would read, I would lock myself into a book as a way of denying reality.

'Towards the end of my time at the community, the leaders kept pushing me towards some kind of reconciliation, because God is a God who reconciles. At first I went into panic mode. But I made contact with my sisters and we tried to arrange for my family to come down to the West Country so we could have a meeting on my territory. But it never actually happened. My grandad in India fell ill, and Mum had to go out there to be with him.

'I was ready to leave, and Tig came down for me. I stayed at her house for a few days. The plan was that I would go back to the polytechnic and live in Coventry. The first place I found there was terrible, and I moved several times. There's nothing more disorientating than wanting a home and a family and not getting one. In the end I had to pack in the course because I couldn't cope with dealing with my own family and the demands of the college work.'

'I trusted God and would never lose that trust'

'At the church I went to in Coventry there was an older couple who set up a meeting at their house with my family. My half-brother came with my sister-in-law, my mum and one of my sisters – the one who had threatened to kill her baby. She arrived wearing a pair of my shoes!

'When we opened the door, Mum just stood there crying. Then they all came inside and sat down, and Mum blamed me for everything. I made it clear that I was perfectly willing to live at home but I didn't want to get married. She had tried to push me into marriage and that was the reason I had left. I told my family that I believed God and trusted God, and would never lose that trust. And that's how the meeting ended.

'Six months later I moved back to Birmingham. I made contact with my sisters again, and we began to build a relationship. I also started visiting home occasionally.

'Now if my sisters need help, they phone me and ask me to pray. I find this amazing. I've witnessed to them and they both know that their options are to go to heaven or to go to hell. They have actually told me that they wish they had done what I've done. They envy me for having my own life and not being at someone else's beck and call.

'In the midst of all this, the only steadfast thing in my life is God. If I had to do what I've done again, I'd do it – though not in exactly the same way; I'd do it with a little more wisdom! But it has certainly made me the person I am today.'

'I've counselled so many people!'

Kal now shares a flat with another Christian girl. She works part-time as a nursery nurse, preparing three- to five-year-olds for school. This leaves her time, and not just to see her friends: 'I've counselled and prayed for so many people!' She has been able to help other Asian girls who have become Christians. Some have managed to stay at home without facing the problems she encountered, and they have seen their whole family turn to Christ. But Kal is aware that there are Asian girls who try to use Christianity simply as an excuse for leaving home.

It is seven years since Kal herself left home. Her school-friend Sue is now a probation officer in the West Midlands area, but they keep in touch. Kal has had ample time to reflect on her own story, a story she retells sometimes with tears, more often with laughter. She has a wonderful sense of humour and a remarkable ability to laugh at her own mistakes.

She realises that what she went through is totally outside the experience of most Christians in this country, though she points out that anyone who has experienced rejection, for whatever reason, would have some empathy with her story. But, seven years on, how does she think that, for example, the Christians in the West Country community could have helped her more?

'White European expectations'

'Because I appeared to be coping – I wasn't crying all the time, although I would in the privacy of my own room – I don't think people realised what a drastic change there had been in my life. I'd been an ordinary Indian girl who lived at home, who did all the cooking and cleaning, who was at the beck and call of her parents. Now I had a completely different life-style. This took a lot of adjusting to.

'And people's expectations of me were white European expectations. For example, they didn't think twice about taking me off to the pub. For me this was so abnormal. I'd never had any desire to go to the pub! They didn't even ask me if I would like to go. They would just say, "Come on! We're all going!" And you either went along and made friends, or you stayed behind and ended up on your own.

'I wasn't seen as Kal, the individual. They were simply saying, "Come and join *us*!" Nobody actually came alongside me to ask, "Are *you* all right? Are *you* coping?"

'People would ask "How are you?" and I'd say "Fine." If I didn't say "Fine", they wouldn't know what to say next.'

'The key is to listen'

'As I've counselled other people, God has taught me that the key is to tune your ear to *listen*, as the scripture says. It wasn't that I didn't want to share – I was desperate to say to someone, "Please help me! I'm in a mess!" Once during house-group the leader asked me if I was OK, and I just cried. And nobody said, "Do you need to talk?" In the end, I just bottled it all up.

'People supported me as far as they were able. I'd get letters from my family that would upset me, and they would gather round and give me a hug. But apart from that, I was expected to carry on as normal. They saw me as a strong Christian because of what I'd done, but in fact I was struggling. It was so very hard.

'Just before I left home, I was diagnosed as having a condition that called for a very strict diet, and I had to take all kinds of iron tablets because my blood count was so low. I knew I had to get myself checked at a local hospital. This was on my mind, as well as all the emotional feelings about leaving home. Sometimes it overwhelmed me and there was nobody to talk to. I know that to talk to someone like me takes time and commitment, but that's what the Christian walk is all about.'

'You can't just share the gospel, then move on'

Remembering Sue, what advice would Kal give to those who find themselves coming alongside an Asian or someone with another faith background? Some Christians in that situation feel they would upset umpteen apple-carts if they were to share their Christian faith.

'People in Sue's position do a phenomenal work. I

would never ever discourage them from spreading the gospel. If it hadn't been for Sue, God only knows where I'd be now. But when you witness to people of other faiths, especially from Asia, remember that for them to change their faith often brings severe consequences. A decision to follow Christ affects their whole family. The cost will be high – though in scripture that is the cost for *everyone*.

'If you share the gospel with someone from another faith background, and they give their life to the Lord, you can't then move on. That person is going to need you so much. Keep them covered in prayer and be there when they need you, especially when the apple-carts do turn over.'

Chapter 3

WHEN THE FLOOD WATERS RISE

When I saw a lifebelt hanging by the entrance to the churchyard in the village where Nira lives, it looked a bit out of place. There didn't seem to be much risk of my drowning. The nearest river was well out of sight across the fields, and the only water I could see was a puddle!

But I found out from Nira that at times the river can surge over its banks, cross the fields and flood parts of the village. That lifebelt isn't such an oddity after all.

Nira's house is above the flood line. She has only recently moved in and is very thrilled with it. She has named it 'YHWH-Jireh'. But more about that later.

Nira grew up in Leicester. She remembers, when she was very young, pouring rice pudding from her high chair onto the family dog. She assures me she did it because she liked the dog and not because she disliked rice pudding. Early in life, she demonstrated her willingness to share.

Too much going on

Nira enjoyed school very much, until she was sixteen. 'I liked achieving. But all at once there was too much to juggle in life and I couldn't keep all the balls in the air.' The family moved to the Lancashire coast. 'I didn't settle into my new grammar school. I was treated as a stranger the whole time I was there. The courses were provided by a different examination board and they didn't match the courses at my previous school at all. It was a nightmare. I didn't get the help I needed, though I suppose I didn't really ask for it.' Nira failed to get the grades she needed for university.

She had worked at a local pharmacy during the school holidays, and wanted to be a pharmacist. She took a job as a trainee pharmacy technician and studied at what is now Preston Polytechnic. 'It was a doddle, very easy work. But I can look back now and see that I wasn't really fulfilling my potential.'

They met at a railway station

She met her husband-to-be at Lancaster railway station on her way to Preston. He was re-taking his A-levels at the college where Nira was studying. 'It was a bitterly cold day. I had a scarf over my nose and there wasn't much he could have seen of me, apart from my eyes.'

Nira's husband-to-be was studying for a Higher National Diploma but not for a degree. This was to prove significant in the story of their life together.

They married two years after that first meeting. 'We moved into a horrendous little flat. It was very, very damp. Water used to run down the walls, and it was overrun with mice. There was a threadbare carpet in one of the rooms. It had probably once been royal blue, but we came back from work one night and found that it had turned white – with fungus!'

Meeting God

By the time their first daughter arrived they had bought a two-up, two-down terraced house. It was then Nira became desperately ill – and met with God.

She had been to Sunday School and had links with church all the time she was growing up. 'I feel that for nearly all my life I have known about the Lord. But I reckon that the point at which I came to know him as my personal

Saviour was when I was in hospital, a few days after the birth of my elder daughter. At the time I had no idea what was wrong with me. I was paralysed.

'A very kind nurse asked if I would like to attend a communion service in the hospital. It was very low-key, very unemotional. I doubt if it lasted more than ten minutes. At the end of it I just dissolved into tears and felt happy – very, very happy. I prayed, "Thank you, Lord, that if anyone is afflicted, it's me and not my baby. Because she's beautiful. I can cope with it better if it's me, not her."

'I felt the Lord saying, "Come on, Nira, I'm fed up with you messing around. It's about time I really knew that you were mine!" This was a key moment.'

However, it was also the point at which Nira's marriage started to go downhill.

She didn't tell her husband about her new commitment to the Lord. 'The significance of it didn't hit me straight away. It took years as I grew in understanding and found people who could help me. I'd gone to church all the time we were engaged – we didn't see each other on Sundays until the afternoon. But once we were married I stopped going. I suppose I realised it wasn't going to be acceptable.'

'My Bible had been put in the dustbin'

Three years after that time in hospital, Nira and her husband moved to another part of North West England. 'By this time we had two daughters. I had no transport but there was a field at the back of our house. Even though I still couldn't walk very far, I could go through our back gate and into the field. I could get away from home, and we could picnic there.

'But the field didn't last long. Three weeks after we moved in, so did the developers. They built thirty-three houses, which was very upsetting. However, the first people to move into one of the new houses were dear Christians, and it was the wife in that family, Ruth, who really helped me to understand what had happened to me. I struggled for a while, wanting to keep my beliefs private. But it was in Ruth's kitchen that I had the experience of being filled with the Spirit.

'Meanwhile, my marriage was becoming even more rocky. If I left Christian books around, it would cause a lot of trouble. One day I even found that my Bible had been put in the dustbin.'

Why was her husband so hostile? 'His parents are churchgoers, and maybe they forced him to go when he was young.' But Nira has come to believe that because of her new allegiance, her husband 'felt demoted, knocked off his pedestal. I couldn't see this when I was younger, but I can see now that he was always a very jealous person, very insecure. He was the youngest of four boys, the youngest by a long way. He knew he wasn't wanted, he knew he was a mistake, and that didn't help.

'He is supposed to be a good manager but he has great difficulty in communicating.

'I started to attend Ruth's church – not very regularly at weekends, but during the week. My health gradually improved and it was real joy to be with such amazing people. They were young, they were alive. My only previous memories of church were going as a child and as a teenager in a town that really only catered for holiday-makers and OAPs!

'An elder at the church's parent fellowship produced excellent Bible teaching tapes, and I played these at home in the daytime. But everything had to be cleared away before my husband came home. I often felt I was living a lie but I couldn't see an answer to it. The church fellowship were very supportive. They encouraged me to stand up to my husband and to come to church more often on Sundays, which I tried to do. But it was very hard.

'Once I took my husband to one of the church's social gatherings. It was Bonfire Night and they were having a party for the children. The children enjoyed it and so did the adults. Somebody talked to my husband about rugby and somebody talked to him about computers. Nobody mentioned the Lord at all.

'Yet we hardly touched less than 100 miles an hour in the car on the way home. I thought my husband would kill us, and it took him weeks to be reasonable to me again.'

'I didn't want to go home'

'I was being treated so badly and.I couldn't believe the Lord wanted me to suffer. I had to get away. I went to the Lake District and stayed in a caravan for a few days. It was Easter and my mother had the children. I went to a little church way up in the hills on Easter Sunday.

'I really didn't want to go home. I decided to visit Ruth, but I had to go past the end of our road. My husband saw me. He was violently angry. He blamed me for everything and demolished any self-confidence I still had.

'We carried on for a few more years. As a Christian, I felt I had to fight for my marriage and fight hard. I prayed an awful lot about it. Then came the point when we moved to the Midlands. My husband's firm wanted him down here. I was reluctant to leave my friends and the fellowship, but we moved.

'We had to live in a caravan until we could move into our house, and we had all the problems of washing the children's clothes in a bucket! But the first person I met in the village was the wife of a local minister, and members of the church rushed round to help. It was a wonderful feeling. I went to the church – again more on weekdays than at weekends.'

'I didn't just read this prospectus, I ate it!'

'Then the Lord sent me to college – that was his doing. We used to go camping in France most summers, and both my daughters had prolonged, six-month exchange visits with French students. They have both been bilingual since they were nine or ten. So I thought I ought to try and catch up by going to French conversation classes, and I sent off for a prospectus.

'The trouble was, I sent off to the wrong college and the prospectus that came back was from the local college of higher education. It was for degrees and wonderfully exciting things like that. I didn't just read that prospectus, I ate it! At the end the college invited you, if you didn't think you were qualified to start on a degree course, to write a quick résumé of who you were and what you'd done, and to send it off. So I did. When I posted the letter, I felt a pat on the back and a "Well done!" I was called for an interview within days, and I was accepted there and then – warts and all! – on a four-year, full-time degree course. I felt so at home. I enjoyed the whole package!'

'He was always putting me down'

During the first six months of her course Nira's husband never spoke to her. He was now bitterly opposed not only to her Christian faith but also to her studying. Not for the first time 'our whole relationship was in difficulty whenever I didn't agree with him about anything!

'He was always putting me down. For example, when we were in the North West, I had run a confectionery business – and had even won a contract with ICI for a fifty-year celebration, but my husband continually told me I couldn't cook or bake.

'When the news came through that I'd got my degree, I phoned to tell him. He was in a meeting with the managing director. But when I explained to the secretary what news I had for him, she said, "Oh, I'll break into the meeting for that!" So she put me through and my husband picked up the phone. "What's the matter?"

'I said, "Nothing's the matter. I've got my degree! I want you to be the first to know."

'He replied in an abrupt tone of voice, "Oh! Very good. I'm busy!" Then the managing director came on the phone and said everything my husband should have said and more.

'After that, my husband more than doubled his efforts to belittle me. He would contradict everything I said. I had gained confidence through doing my degree and he accused me of being aggressive. Part of the problem was, he only had a Higher National Diploma. But I'd studied because I thought it would be for the good of the family. If I could teach for a couple of days a week, it would help with the family budget.

'We went camping in France again that summer, and I think it was while we were there that I became aware I wasn't the only one he was undermining. He was putting our daughters down too.'

'You can't go on like this'

'Things got worse and worse. I asked my husband for a trial separation, but he refused point blank. I moved my stuff out of the bedroom and slept on the settee. I decided to go and see a solicitor, but first I went to a local minister to ask for advice. He looked me straight in the eye and said he believed the Lord was telling me I was making a big mistake. I was absolutely flabbergasted.'

Nira couldn't believe that a Christian could be so insensitive and show so little understanding of what she had been through. 'I felt he was undermining my relationship with the Lord. I believed strongly that the Lord was supporting me and didn't want me to go on being so unhappy. And there were the repercussions on the children. They weren't just my children, they were *ours*.'

Her solicitor gave her very different advice. She recommended divorce. 'You can't go on like this, Nira,' she said. 'You have tried so many times to make your marriage work. A separation would not be enough to contain your husband. You need to have the strength of the courts behind you.'

Freedom

Nira discovered that her husband had had 'innumerable affairs'. He didn't contest the divorce, and one day Nira had a letter in the post to say it had been finalised and she had gained her freedom. The date of the decree absolute was the fourth of July, American Independence Day. This made her laugh, something she never thought she would do under the circumstances. She recognised that on that day the Lord had taken away the trauma and turmoil of the past.

'I claimed this house'

Sorting out the practical and financial aspects of the divorce proved a frustratingly slow and painful process, and still continues a year later.

The house above the flood line had been on the market for two and a half years. Nira put in an offer for it three times and lost it twice. It was sold to someone else but they couldn't get their finances together.

'I used to park close by here when I was on my way to church' – the church with the lifebelt at the entrance to its churchyard – 'and I claimed this house in the name of Jesus Christ.' Now Nira has her house above the flood line. It's home for her, her daughters and their dog and cat. She named it 'YHWH-Jireh' because she wants everyone to know it was God's provision.

When she applied for her part-time teaching job, Nira made no secret of either her Christian faith or her divorce. She was accepted, and it is a job she enjoys. But how have her daughters reacted to the break-up of her marriage?

'Mainly they have been very supportive. They're old enough now to understand something of what was going on. You can't hide things from young children and you certainly can't hide them from teenagers. Now that things are further down the road, they have started to see their father again, very occasionally.

'It's early yet in the healing process. My elder daughter is a very gentle, very spiritual person, with a real Christian commitment. She has forgiven her father for what he's done. I'm delighted about this – but it hurts too.

'My younger daughter has some of her father's ways and I wrestle with that at times. But now she, too, has accepted Jesus as her Saviour.

'I've tried not to bombard them with all the details of the divorce but I've also tried to keep them up-to-date. It's a very fine line to draw, and I've gone wrong on both sides. But I've got some of it right with the Lord's help.'

'I argued with the Lord all night'

Support and encouragement have come from outside her family. One evening, when she was in the midst of the divorce trauma, Nira went to a meeting for people from various local churches. That night schools worker Andrew Smith 'bounced onto the platform with great energy and enthusiasm. He surprised us by starting his spiel for the evening by announcing they were desperate to find a cook for one of Scripture Union's holidays for young people.

'I felt the Lord saying to me, "It's you!" But I said, "Lord, I can't! I've got too much to do. I'm in the middle of all this trauma!" I lay awake through the night arguing with the Lord about it. But in the morning I rang up Andrew to tell him he had got himself a cook.'

So off Nira went to the holiday at Colwyn Bay on the North Wales coast. Cooking was no problem to her and she was able to exercise what she has long regarded as her God-given gift as a confectioner. But there was more than that for her on the holiday.

Appreciation and love

She found the Christian fellowship indescribable. 'I was hurting desperately. I'd been treated like dirt for years and years. My confidence had been knocked right down. My cooking had never been appreciated. Not once in our married life had my husband said, "I really enjoyed that!" Yet there on the holiday at Colwyn Bay – hour in, hour out, day in, day out – there was appreciation and love by the bucketful. What a confidence booster! It was just what I needed. I knew why the Lord had told me, "You're going to get off that chair and you're going to do it!"

'I was able to share with the leaders what this love and acceptance meant to me. I could see from their faces how much they appreciated what I was saying to them.'

During the holiday Nira struck up a friendship with Andrew's colleague, Gill Hutchinson. 'This friendship led to my being invited to join the prayer group supporting Gill in her schools ministry. I was absolutely over the moon to be asked to join.'

'The rivers will not sweep over you'

Nira has found herself on the receiving end of love from so many Christians. 'That love has been shown in a lot of ways. A touch on the arm, or "I've made a few extra mince pies and I can't get them all in my tin. You can use them, can't you?" Some people have just been there to lend a listening ear. And when there was no money... I could go on and on!'

Nira has found love and acceptance, and found them in abundance. 'I'm glad to say that I can now talk freely, even to the minister who was so unhelpful to me.'

Nira's house is above the flood line, but this hasn't been true of her life. Instead, she has proved the truth of God's promise in the book of Isaiah: 'When you pass through the waters, I will be with you; and when you pass through the rivers, they will not sweep over you.'

Chapter 4

THOUSANDS OF CHILDREN

Like many pensioners, Reg has a computer. His father was
the last man in Tetbury in Gloucestershire to drive a horse-
drawn mail van. Such has been the pace of change in this
century. His wife Gladys remembers electricity arriving in
her childhood home in Weymouth. Until then it had been lit
by oil lamps and candles.

Her father was a Cornishman. He had been a chief engi-
neer in the Navy and worked at a torpedo factory. She had
five sisters and a brother, and they regularly attended the
local Church of England Sunday School in Weymouth. She
remembers going to mid-week children's meetings and
singing choruses like 'Wide, wide as the ocean' and 'All the
way to Calvary'.

'I thought I was a Christian but I wasn't. I didn't realise
that until a few years later.'

'So Father could keep his eye on us'

In those days, fathers could rule their families with an auto-
cratic hand. 'When war came,' says Gladys, 'I really wanted
to join the services, but Father wouldn't allow any of his
daughters to join.' After leaving school, Gladys went to
work in Woolworth's. 'I was one of the window-trimmers,
as they used to call them.' And, when the time came for her
and her sisters to do some kind of war work, they went into
a local factory 'so Father could keep his beady eye on us.

'After the war ended, I thought I'd go back to my old job at Woolworth's, but they wanted me to go to the North of England. I wasn't willing, so I was out of work for five or six weeks.' That must have seemed like a lifetime in those days of full employment.

However, one day her mother met the Superintendent of the local NAAFI (Navy, Army and Air Force Institutes which ran canteens for service personnel), which was at the White Ensign Club in Weymouth. He enquired after the girls. When he heard she was out of work, he said, 'I'll give Gladys a job any day.' So she went to work in the restaurant.

Reg was the NAAFI's under-manager, but was promoted to the manager's job. He needed his meals in his office, so Gladys used to take them in…

In Tetbury, Reg's family worshipped with the Christian Brethren, whose assembly had been started the previous century through the interest of George Muller of Bristol, famous for his homes for orphan children. There was a very large Sunday School and Reg had an abundance of Christian teaching. 'Much of it may appear to have gone over my head, but I think I learned more than I realised.'

When Reg left school, he went into the grocery trade. Then the war came. 'My father wanted me to be a conscientious objector, but I didn't feel I could be. So I volunteered to go into the NAAFI in the Navy and was given the uniform of a Naval Petty Officer. I served in Russia for fifteen months – I was based mainly in Archangel. But I was in Weymouth and Portland for D-Day and, as the war ended, I came back to Weymouth – and met Gladys.

'When I first saw her, I thought she was a very nice girl. But as she wasn't a Christian I had no thoughts of inviting her out.'

Conversation in the canteen

One day Reg asked Gladys to go on duty at the NAAFI
while he went out for the evening to a church service.
'When he got back, I asked him, "Did you have a nice service?" He began to tell me all about it. He said, "Are you a
Christian?" So I said, "Oh, yes! Of course I am!" Then I
realised I wasn't – but I didn't tell him that.

'Some while later, he told me there was a mission at his
church. I went along but I didn't tell him I was going. On
the last night the preacher spoke just as if he was talking to
me personally. He quoted the Bible verse, "All have
sinned…" He said, "When the Lord Jesus comes, if you
haven't put your faith in him, you'll be left behind for
judgement. You won't go to heaven with him." That made
me think.

'I wanted to go to the same church next Sunday, but
Mother wasn't keen because it wasn't C of E. But being just
over twenty-one I was able to please myself.'

Twenty past seven on the corner by the statue

'When I came out of the service, a young lady touched my
arm. Her name was Margaret Wilkins, and she invited me to
a Bible class on the following Friday night. I said, "Thank
you, but I belong to the C of E and I don't want to join any
other group." She said, "Just in case you change your mind,
I'll meet you at twenty past seven on the corner by the
statue."

'All that week I thought, *Shall I go?* When it came to
Friday night, I decided I'd go along to the corner to see if
she was there. And she was. When she saw me, she just
beamed.

'The meeting was held in a private house and the lady of
the house, Miss Vera Conway, gave the message. I started
going every week and, in the meantime, I'd been talking to
Reg. One Friday night I was so convicted, I knelt down and

gave my heart to the Lord Jesus.'

Reg had entertained no thoughts of inviting Gladys out because she wasn't a believer, but now God had wonderfully stepped in…

Leaving a shop that sold delicious cream cakes

Reg proposed to Gladys in the gardens of the Swan Marina. They were married and together they managed a shop selling delicious cream cakes. Reg enjoyed business life but he was also very active in Christian work. He realised that one or the other would have to go. 'I was working with children and I was busy preaching. I spoke at open air meetings along Weymouth sea front. One time I thought God was calling me to St Lucia in the West Indies – I had met a missionary from there. But Gladys can't stand much of the heat.'

They continued working in the shop in Weymouth for ten years. Then Reg saw two films which were shown by the Secretary of the Counties Evangelistic Work. 'After the second meeting, I tentatively spoke to him. He rather swept the ground from under my feet. It so happened that the Counties evangelist for Hertfordshire was just about to go off to the Philippines. So the Secretary arranged for me to go down to Kent for an interview. Afterwards, when we were about to drive home in the car, he said to Gladys, "See that he doesn't turn back!"

'We drove a little way away and then stopped and had a word of prayer. I can't describe the peace that came over me then. That peace was with me all the way back to Weymouth.'

Thus it was in 1958 that Reg and Gladys left the cream cakes behind to embark on more than thirty-five years of ministry with Counties, as the Counties Evangelistic Work is now more briefly known. Counties has its roots in the Christian Brethren but works with other churches too, though it is still sponsored and largely supported by Brethren assemblies.

Reg was given no specific training for his work as an evangelist. It wasn't as customary then as it is now to ask prospective 'full-time' evangelists to go to Bible college. But Reg asserts that business life provides a good training in human relationships. Moreover, he became a full-time Christian worker only after his gifts as an evangelist had been recognised and developed not only inside church buildings but among the crowds of holidaymakers on Weymouth seashore.

Life under canvas

In their early days with Counties, most of their meetings were held in a tent, and they made do with a caravan for their living quarters. Their first tent mission was in Hatfield, opposite the Odeon cinema. During the autumn, winter and spring they would conduct evangelistic crusades by invitation in many parts of the British Isles. They also ran youth camps for young people in the 11–18 age-range. Initially they would have a week's camp for a hundred boys and then another for a hundred girls. Later the camps were mixed.

They lived in their caravan for all of their first eighteen months with Counties. Then a wealthy friend invited them to share his home and they stayed with him for the next six years. Reg and Gladys moved into their present flat on a neat, leafy local authority estate in Hemel Hempstead in 1965. But some of their happiest days have been spent under canvas.

Camp life brought with it its hazardous and often hilarious moments. Once, when they were sleeping in a fairly elderly bell tent, there was a tremendous storm and the tent collapsed on them in the middle of the night. And they cheerfully tell the story of the very neat, precise lady who accidentally fell into the refuse pit.

To quote a Scripture Union youth worker in Australia, Christian camps are 'temporary Christian communities' where the gospel can be demonstrated as well as proclaimed. Reg and Gladys have many memories of those who came to faith in Christ at their camps. 'We are still in touch today with large numbers of young people, some of them in the mission field.

'Our tent missions through the year would be times of sowing; our summer camps would be times of reaping. But you have to be a little careful lest you create a hothouse atmosphere at a camp. In their enthusiasm, young Christians may be over-zealous in trying to get other young people to make professions of faith.'

Pioneering family camps

Reg and Gladys were probably amongst the first Christian leaders in Britain to run family camps. Reg had been to America several times and seen family camps over there, and he had been very impressed. Their first one – 'a small camp, just sixty people' – took place fifteen years after their first youth camp.

These camps were particularly geared towards families where the wife was a believer and the husband was not, or vice versa. 'We saw families united in the Lord.' Families who were entirely non-Christian also came, brought along by Christian friends.

'We had a wide age range, from nought to well over fifty. We had grandparents there, and we often found that children who were converted to Christ had Christian grandparents who had been praying for them.

'Families brought their own caravans or tents to sleep in. At youth camps we did all the catering, but at family camps everyone did their own. However, on a couple of afternoons we would all come together and share our tea. And after the evening session we provided tea, coffee, cocoa and biscuits.

One night we would do baked potatoes in their jackets, and another we would have a midnight (or nearly midnight) swim. That was always very popular.'

Family values

Morning sessions – one for adults, one for teenagers and one for children – consisted mostly of Bible teaching. Reg also remembers a series of talks on family values, in which the speaker explained the relationship between the three Persons of the Trinity. 'He pointed out that the Father, the Son and the Holy Spirit are all equal, and yet the Lord Jesus subordinated himself to the Father, and the Holy Spirit to the Lord Jesus. And he applied this to family relationships.'

Evening sessions were evangelistic, for all ages together. Occasionally there would be a film, and sometimes the local villagers would join in. During the day families went off on their own or in groups, but there was one day of organised games and an outing which they all went on together.

Reg was a staff evangelist with Counties for thirty-two years, and even after he retired at the age of sixty-five he continued to look after some of their Bible Exhibitions. Looking back, he says he would do it all again.

God's presence

Today he is still preaching, still sharing the gospel, despite a number of illnesses. 'When I was fifty-one, I tried to push a lady's car – she had her wheel turned into the kerb. That night I had a heart attack and was taken to hospital.

'Ten years later I had another heart attack. I was playing a game at camp. I was very foolish.'

The game was crocker, an ultra-energetic variation on cricket which you play with a football. If you hit the football, or even if you don't, you have to run to what in cricket would be the square-leg position and back, before the bowler can bowl the ball again and hit your stumps. So far as I know, it is a game that is peculiar (some would say in both senses) to Christian youth organisations. It is definitely not recommended for over-fifties, and certainly not for those with any history of heart disease.

Nor is that all. Ten years ago Reg had an operation for cancer of the bowel and a colostomy which was later reversed. He has also undergone a prostate operation and, three years ago, five heart bypasses at St Mary's Hospital in London. In and through all these trials Reg says, 'The Lord has been very gracious.

'I remember after my first heart attack – my mother was still alive then – she sent me a letter with a little calendar tab on which was printed, "God is my salvation. I will trust and not be afraid. The Lord is my strength and my song" (Isaiah 12:2). I shared my mother's letter with the nurse in the intensive-care ward.

'I've experienced the Lord's presence all through these operations. I've learned more about him during those times than at any others.'

No children?

'We've had no children – Gladys had a number of operations which prevented this. We would have loved children of our own and we did wonder whether we should adopt. But we felt the Lord was calling us into Christian work we were better equipped to do because we had no children.

'Our life has been a very fulfilling one. We have met thousands of children, in villages and on large housing estates. Through them we have been able to meet their parents.'

'We have had the joy of sharing in other people's children,' says Gladys. 'One friend of ours has had six, and every time she had a new baby she would let me cuddle it.'

Reg adds, 'Gladys could enjoy other people's children

without a trace of jealousy. We know a couple who have no children, and sadly today they seem far away from the Lord. I think that having no children has been their main problem. They didn't seek to fill their lives with something else that could have been a blessing to them.'

'As enthralling as coconut shies'

Reg and Gladys have had a lot of fun. I was shown a book of press cuttings, which records that a nearby circus once turned down its music so Reg could hear himself preach. 'In return,' said the reporter, 'Reg and Gladys tried out a dodgem for size. And,' he added, 'the children of Kimpton did not confine their interests to the coconut shies. They found Reg's Happy Hour Rallies in the tent every bit as enthralling.'

More than friends

Reg and Gladys have neither children nor grandchildren, yet their lives have been and still are packed with friends – packed to overflowing because, over the years, they have always been willing to offer friendship, sometimes costly friendship, in the name of Christ.

Nor, of course, are their friends just friends: they are members of the family of Christian believers. Reg and Gladys treasure past memories of the people they have met. They display some of their photographs in their living room, keep in touch with them and pray for them. Many of these friends might not belong to God's family at all, had not God given Reg and Gladys the courage and the love to share the good news so widely. Their faithfulness has brought them all the family they could wish for. No wonder they feel a sense of fulfilment.

Chapter 5

'I'VE TAKEN RESPONSIBILITY
FOR WHAT I'VE DONE'

'I went through the front door and thought, *This is my house!*'

So Helen bought the two-up, two-down Victorian semi, just up the road from the church and from what was to be Jack's school, in a suburb of Southampton.

She enjoys her house, particularly the pine floor in her dining-room. Her father thinks it would be warmer if she had a carpet. She doesn't agree, though she admits that one day she may change her mind. She also loves her new wooden window-frames. 'Dad thought I ought to have PVC windows, but I know what I want and he's learnt not to interfere.'

Helen grew up in Southampton and became a committed Christian when she was fourteen or fifteen. 'I started off in a funny sort of house church which I didn't much like. I didn't feel comfortable with the way they worshipped – there was a lot of dancing. If I'm happy, that's not the way I express myself.

'I was actually very lonely in the church, partly because I was never quite sure what was going on. It seemed so far removed from everyday life that I couldn't make much sense of it. And I was also quite shy. The irony is that you can feel desperately lonely in a place where you're supposed to feel quite the opposite. But very few people will admit this.'

Ordinary Christians

'When I said I was going to leave, they did everything they could to stop me. They said there would be "no freedom of the Spirit at that other church". And I thought, *If you really loved people, you wouldn't be doing this to me.*'

Despite the pressure, she did leave to go to a very different style of church, Above Bar, with two of her school friends. She was relieved to find that the people there were 'ordinary' and seemed more in touch with everyday life.

When she left school, Helen went north to Leeds University. 'I loved Leeds. I can remember getting off the train and going out into the city square thinking, *This place is alive!* I found it quite frightening but I loved it all the same.

'There was so much going on. In Leeds people seem to provide their own entertainment, whereas in Southampton you just wait until somebody lays something on.'

Her progress towards her degree was not without interruptions. 'I started getting panic attacks. I was told these were the result of bad breathing habits caused by prolonged periods of stress, and I felt I had to sort this out. So I took a year out.

'I went to work in a local bookshop, alongside the wife of the manager of what was then the Scripture Union bookshop in Leeds. She and her husband worshipped at the same church as I did, St George's. When the bookshop closed down, I was taken on at the Scripture Union shop. I worked there, on and off, during the summer holidays and for a year after I had finished my degree.'

Living in an unreal world?

Helen wasn't altogether impressed by some of the customers she met in the shop. In her view, a lot of them were living in an unreal world. 'They thought they were being Christians just by reading Christian books and listening to Graham Kendrick all the time.'

One aspect of the evangelical subculture that particularly irritated her was the sale of 'Christian' knick-knacks – trinkets, erasers with Bible texts on them, and all the rest. 'It was as if having these things around the house would make you that little bit more Christian, which isn't true.'

Back on her degree course, she went abroad with other students, first to France and then to Italy. She had found the bookshop restricting, so going abroad was like a breath of fresh air. 'We had a wonderful time in France, at the university in Caen in Normandy.'

Padua in Italy proved a very different experience. It had a major drugs problem and their accommodation was less than adequate. They were also up against the attitudes of the local Italian women, who all seemed to be wearing designer clothes. 'We were always in jeans. You would get on a bus and ten pairs of female eyes would look you up and down in absolute disgust as if to say, *What is that tramp doing on this bus?'*

A bad year

Helen returned to her beloved Leeds and lived quite near St George's Church. But she had what she describes as 'a bit of a bad year'.

'My parents hit a difficult patch, and I was still getting panic attacks. Then after my graduation, while I was staying with my sister in Devon, I was involved in a car accident. Some of my vertebrae were crushed, and I spent six months doing nothing, with various contraptions round my neck.'

She also faced a not unusual problem: what do you do with a languages degree if you don't want to teach? 'My mum is a teacher and she always used to say that Liz (that's my sister) would make a great teacher. But she didn't think I would. But teaching isn't a job that appeals to me, so I didn't need much discouraging.'

She solved her problem in the short term by going back on the staff of the Scripture Union bookshop, in the January after her graduation. (They had kept the job open for her until she had recovered from the car crash and could return to Leeds.) She left the shop the following November.

'The most excruciating moment of my life'

'I was fed up with the claustrophobic atmosphere at church. People there seemed very constricted by rules, and I'm just a bit headstrong.' Helen obviously finds it hard to cope with friends who start preaching at her. 'I knew other people who I could trust not to do this and with whom I could be completely myself. I was leading a bit of a double life really...

'The most excruciating moment of my life was when I had to tell the manager of the shop I was pregnant. It was one Saturday morning, and he and I were alone in the shop. He began to talk about holidays, and I had to tell him that I wouldn't be entitled to one because I would be leaving to have a baby. To this day I still wonder what on earth went on in his mind. But he and the others were very nice to me. When I left, Scripture Union overpaid me by a week by mistake. I told them about it, but they sent me a nice letter saying I probably needed the money more than they did and they didn't want it back. I've always been grateful for that.'

How did her parents react to the news? 'Mum was really pleased that one of her daughters had done something unconventional. She told Dad. He never really said anything but he didn't get cross. Now both Mum and Dad help to look after Jack.'

'If ever you need any help...'

'The leaders at St George's were all very supportive. I'll never forget the time when one of the curates came up to me and said, "If ever you need any help..." That was so nice, I felt like crying.

'When I was pregnant, I used to go along to the mums' group at church after work. But I knew another girl who'd had a son when she was at university, and her church in Lancashire had excommunicated her. She was very upset by that and never really got over it. To their credit, nobody at St George's was like that at all.

'The only person who condemned me was an old lady who came up and asked in broad Yorkshire, "Are you married?" When I said I wasn't, she said, "You should be!"

'I replied, "How rude!" in my best southern accent.'

Meanwhile, the panic attacks continued. 'It was hard – not wanting to go out on my own or on long journeys because I was afraid of what might happen. It was also hard because Jesus was supposed to have the answer and appeared not to. I remember going to the mums' group and feeling how ridiculous it was to sit there with my mouth shut when they asked for items for prayer, when I had this massive problem which made going out of the door every day a struggle.'

Helen never considered having an abortion. 'Jack's father would have liked me to, but very early on – even before I was sure I was pregnant – I had this dream of myself on a bus with a baby. After that dream I felt I knew the baby, and there was no way I could have had an abortion. Also, I knew a couple of people who had had abortions and they were really screwed up, especially when they looked at children who were the same age as theirs would have been.

'As for marriage, even if Jack's father and I had stayed together, somehow it never occurred to me that we might get married, though we're still in touch.'

'I could see people going up the church steps'

Jack was born in Leeds in the hospital right next to St George's. 'I went into labour on a Sunday morning and, as

I did so, I looked through the window and could see people going up the church steps.

'After Jack was born, I went to stay with his other grandparents, then I came south and lived with Mum and Dad for a while. I landed a job as a translator – a local translation agency was looking for someone who knew Italian and who could also help in the office. I've studied for my Diploma in Translation. I enjoy the job and it fits in well with Jack.

'Landing a job made it easier for me to buy a house. Mum and I were driving down the road when we saw this one for sale.' Helen knew at once it was the house for her.

She had worried that she might feel lonely and insecure living on her own with Jack, but she has good neighbours, some of them friends she can call on in an emergency. There is a Neighbourhood Watch Scheme in the road, which organises a number of social events, including an annual bonfire party.

'Since I moved back to Southampton, a counsellor has helped me to accept that I can only be as I am, I can't be anything else – and this has unknotted me considerably. I've begun to accept and even rejoice in the God-given thing that is naturally me!

'The wooden window-frames were a part of this process. It's only recently I've begun challenging my father's advice – and the pleasure I get from looking at those windows!

'I still don't breathe properly, but now I do actually feel happy.'

A friend from the past

'I had just moved in and was stripping the ghastly orange stain off my front door, when there, staring up from the local paper I'd laid on the floor, was a picture of Paul Fenton. I'd known Paul in Leeds when he was doing a course at the polytechnic and he rented a room in the house of some friends of mine. I had got to know him better when I was pregnant because he was friendly with my housemates.'

The newspaper told her that Paul had moved into the area to be Scripture Union schools worker in Hampshire. So Helen rang up Scripture Union's national office for his telephone number, and made contact.

Paul came to see her, and during the visit Helen mentioned she would like to get involved with Scripture Union again. She has always remembered that letter about her extra week's pay, and is 'grateful to Scripture Union for not making my life a misery when I had to leave the bookshop'.

Paul invited Helen to join the catering team at the 'Growth into Leadership' holiday he leads. She accepted, and was back on the team again the following year. She has Paul's prayer diary on the wall above her kitchen sink in the house that no longer has an orange-stained front door.

More than a caterer

'Growth into Leadership' is a holiday for older teenagers but a number of the leaders come with their young children, so Jack has friends to play with. What's more, Paul's wife Nicky runs special activities for the children. 'It's safe, and there aren't many exciting places to go when you're on your own with a child. We have a really good time. And there's a swimming pool.'

There are various styles of worship in the programme. Helen finds some of the meetings very hard. 'I'm more at home with the quieter devotional meetings than when people are clapping their hands and dancing around.'

In Paul's view, Helen contributes far more to the holiday than just catering. And, as countless volunteers at Christian holidays have found, you seem to get back far more than you give.

When the holiday is over, Helen goes back to living alone with Jack, to being the proverbial 'single parent'. 'They've been brilliant about this at work, but my mum has told me that certain of her friends disapprove of me. But I've taken responsibility for what I've done. These things happen. You make mistakes and you live with them. I could have done far worse. But I do appreciate that it would have been much harder without the love and support of my family and friends.'

Many women prefer to live alone

Helen has been surprised at the number of women who say they prefer to live alone. 'Somebody said to me, "At least you can spend your money on what you like, and decorate your house how you like!" Of course, there are advantages and disadvantages. A lot of my friends are single and, if I'm feeling fed up, they understand why. I wouldn't have chosen to be on my own. It was Jack's dad who opted out and made the final decision.'

Mindful of the comments of some politicians, Helen also points out, 'I'm a taxpayer. I pay National Insurance. I'm not sponging. And my friends who are on their own are all working. I wouldn't want not to be working.

'My days are quite full of people, so I do like it when I've put Jack to bed and I've got an evening here on my own and I can just sit. I was worried when I moved here that I'd be alone and isolated. In fact, it's almost the opposite. But sometimes I think it would be nice to be with someone I didn't have to tell how I feel.'

'What would stay with me wherever I was'

Helen is on the committee of an after-school club that looks after children whose parents work. It functions between the end of school and 6pm, and is held in the church centre. Helen is the admissions officer. 'It's quite lot of work, but it's worth it. Jack doesn't actually go yet, because he's only four.'

Helen and Jack attend the 9.30 service at church. 'On a

Sunday morning that's early and we're usually about two minutes late! A lot of people I know stopped going to church when they left university. I didn't. I knew what it was that would stay with me wherever I was.' She attended a house-group for a while but has found it difficult to get babysitters.

She is sorry she doesn't feel in touch with what's going on at church the way she did at St George's in Leeds. 'A lot of this is coloured by my experience when Jack was little. The children leave half way through the service, and I often had to go out with him and miss the sermon. Yet you couldn't easily drift away from this church because it's so well integrated into the community, and Jack's school is a church school.'

'No easy answer'

It's a flourishing, evangelical Anglican church with the problem of success. There are three Sunday morning services and Helen feels it can be a bit like a conveyor belt, 'as if you've got to get the sermon over so that the next service can move in.

'I think people feel more relaxed in the evenings, but 6.30 is bath time and putting-to-bed time for children like Jack. Child-oriented and family-oriented services tend to have a "Noddy" quality, but I don't know that there is an easy answer to that.

'Somebody at my church in Leeds, who was also my doctor when I was a student, rang me when she heard I was pregnant. She said how difficult it was to have children even when you were trying, so there must be some purpose in Jack's existence. I think God's ways are different from our expectations. If anything, I would have expected things to go badly wrong for me after I had Jack, as a sort of retribution for my living my life the "wrong" way. But everything – my house, my job, my friends – has fallen beautifully into place, in stark contrast with the bumpy ride of the pre-Jack years. As I get to know God better, I realise I know him less.'

Chapter 6

'I CAN'T FIND ANY HOLES
IN HIS HEART'

The reds, blues and yellows of a slide, a swing and a climbing frame dominate Deb and Gary's back garden. Gary has started to build an extension to the house, to give the children a large play-room.

Deb was born in the North London suburb of Finchley. Her family moved out to Bletchley in Buckinghamshire when she was two and a half, and she has lived there ever since.

Like many hundreds of others, Deb's mother was born again in another North London district – Harringay. For it was here, during Billy Graham's first major Crusade in Britain in 1954, that she committed her life to Christ.

Deb went regularly to Sunday School when she was growing up, but when she was fourteen she decided – like many teenagers – that she wouldn't attend church any more. By the time she was sixteen she felt she was missing out. 'I began to feel that church on a Sunday morning got my week off to a good start.'

Everybody's friend

Deb had many good Christian friends at church. Petronelle, in particular, stands out. 'She was around when I was a child and she's still around now. She is everybody's friend, always there for anyone who needs her. She officially retired some years ago, but she's doing as much as she ever did.'

Deb loved school. But 'I never told any of the teachers I went to church or that I was a Christian. I wasn't ashamed of it, I just kept it quiet. I had one friend who occasionally came to church, so she knew.'

When Deb left school, she took up a secretarial career. She worked locally for a couple of years and then took a job with the British Medical Association in London. 'At first I hated the commuting, but Mum persuaded me to try it for three months – and before the three months were up I had been promoted.' She stayed with the BMA for eight years, doing 'everything from making coffee to computer graphics'. She also helped experts who were beginning to investigate AIDS. In the end she left to have a baby.

An arranged marriage – in Buckinghamshire?

Gary also comes from a family of Londoners who moved out to Bletchley. His family had no interest in the Christian faith until Gary's brother was killed in a car crash. Gary was twenty at the time.

Ian Pusey, the Rector of St Mary's, went round to see the family and offer comfort. Gary's dad liked Ian and decided to go along to church to see what it was all about. He persuaded Gary's mum to go along, too. Within a year they were both committed Christians, and later Gary's dad had quite a long spell as one of the churchwardens.

But Gary played football, which was his life. He didn't have time for church.

Arranged marriages are doubtless more common in Bombay than in Buckinghamshire, and I suppose Deb and Gary's marriage wasn't exactly arranged. But it was certainly encouraged. 'For years and years,' says Deb (perhaps exaggerating slightly), 'Gary's dad kept saying to me, "You'd like my Gary."' One night there was a barn dance at church, and my boyfriend let me down. Gary was there, and his dad introduced us and left us together.' That night

Gary's mum said, 'Those two are going to get married', and within three weeks Gary had proposed to Deb and she had said yes. Eighteen months later they were married.

'By that time I had a lot of close Christian friends, and one or two of them were saying, "Are you sure you're doing the right thing?" Gary told me, "On Sundays you go to church and I play football. I won't stop you going to church, and you won't stop me playing football." But I thought, *I'll work on him!*'

Her hope and prayer was that, sooner or later, family history would repeat itself. For it was in 1980 – nearly thirty years after her mother had come to faith during Billy Graham's Harringay Crusade – that her father, finally deciding he would go along to church and investigate Christianity for himself, came to faith too.

But Deb began to see her prayers answered rather more quickly…

Part of the Christian family

'When we were expecting Megan, our first child, Gary insisted that he didn't want the baby christened. I was adamant and wouldn't give in. The month before she was born he said, "OK, we'll have the baby christened – and I'd like to be as well."

'He wanted to be part of the Christian family. He hasn't got as far as total commitment yet. He needs to learn more. When he's around, he comes to church. But he works long and strange hours. He builds exhibition stands, sometimes at the National Exhibition Centre in Birmingham or across the Channel in Paris.

'I was twenty-six when Megan was born. Suddenly you're handed this totally defenceless bundle who relies on you for absolutely everything. I didn't know where to start. It was terrifying.

'And she wasn't well. They thought she had meningitis.

So my baby was whipped away from me with a temperature of 104° when she was only two days old. I didn't think I would ever pray as hard again as I prayed that day. But I *have* done since. I've learnt a lot since I gave up one career and started another.'

Megan recovered and the arrival of their second daughter, Olivia, presented no problems at all.

Then came Jacob. 'For the first few days everything was fantastic. But by the eighth and ninth days he was becoming quieter and sleepier, and he wouldn't feed. On the tenth day we called out the doctor at nine o'clock in the evening.' He immediately arranged for Jacob to be taken to Milton Keynes Hospital. He suspected he might have meningitis or pneumonia.

Jacob was given a lumbar puncture, put in an oxygen tank and monitored every fifteen minutes throughout the night. At 5 o'clock the next morning he was given an electrocardiogram to probe the condition of his heart, which they discovered wasn't coping with the needs of his body.

Ambulance dash down the M1

The decision was taken to rush Jacob to the Royal Brompton Hospital in London. At 8 o'clock the ambulance arrived and drove them down the M1, in the rush hour, with a police escort all the way. 'We did the journey in fifty-five minutes at unbelievable speed. They stopped the traffic from Staples Corner in North London right through to the Brompton Road.

'As we sat in the ambulance I said to Gary, "He's going to die." But Gary said, "No, he's not. He'll be OK." Usually I'm the positive one. I can remember praying, *God, if you're going to take him, take him now before I fall in love with him any more.*'

They operated on Jacob that afternoon and discovered that his blood supply had been reaching his brain but not the rest of his body. There were so many holes in his heart, they couldn't even consider patching them.

'Our GP is a Christian and he was able to relay information to our friends. Everyone at St Mary's prayed for Jacob, and so it seems did people in almost every church in Bletchley and Milton Keynes, and in other churches where we have friends.'

After two days Jacob came out of intensive care. After another two he was back in Milton Keynes Hospital, and seven days later he was home.

The doctors hoped the small holes in Jacob's heart would heal. Then they could patch the big ones, though this would leave scar tissue.

'I've looked and looked...'

'A year later we took Jacob back to the Royal Brompton Hospital for a check-up. The consultant seemed to take ages examining him. Finally, he came upstairs and told us, "I can't find any holes at all in his heart."

'We said, "We don't understand..."

'He said, "I've looked and looked and looked, and I still can't find any..."

'If that isn't proof of answered prayer...!' says Deb.

Jacob has to go back to hospital for one more major operation, but he is a bright, lively ginger-haired youngster, cheerfully playing and demanding the occasional biscuit as we talked. 'Look at him now,' says Deb. 'You'd never think there was ever anything wrong.'

An appeal

Deb and Gary felt that the hospitals and the police had treated them so well, the best way to say 'Thank you' was to do something to help people going through the same experience, 'who might not have the faith and the back-up we had'.

They discovered that if Milton Keynes Hospital had had the monitoring equipment needed to measure the oxygen flow in Jacob's blood, they could have checked him at birth before his condition became life-threatening. So they decided to try to raise the money for this key piece of equipment.

They launched their appeal on the day of Jacob's christening. Afterwards, a hundred and twenty of their friends and relations met together at their home. It must have been a fairly tight fit! According to Deb they told their guests, 'You're not getting out of here until...'

They set out to raise the money for one monitor. In fact, they raised enough for three. The Brownies and the Sunday School collected money. Children raised pennies by doing jobs at home. People at the church organised a 'praise' concert. Some local schools gave their Harvest Festival donations. Other local churches and play groups organised collections, too, and envelopes with donations were stuffed through Deb and Gary's letter-box.

Four months after the launch of the appeal, a cheque for £3,000 was presented to a paediatrician from the hospital at a service at St Mary's Church. 'We wanted to do it there because so many of the church family had contributed.'

'Each monitor has a plaque, and we were asked to come up with an inscription for them. Every time I pick Jacob up, I think of the chorus, "Give thanks with a grateful heart", particularly the words, "for now let the weak say 'I am strong'..." So those are the words we chose.'

Amidst all the trauma, did they ever ask why? 'Constantly,' Deb replies. 'I didn't drink during my pregnancy and I don't smoke. The doctors say they just don't know what goes wrong in 95 percent of these cases. We believe there is a reason but we don't fully understand it at the moment. At least we have managed to raise the money for the hospital.'

When friends don't know what to say...

People often don't know what to say to friends who are going through this kind of trauma. 'Some people even crossed the road to avoid having to say anything. My closest friends at church found it very difficult to talk to me. One of them in particular didn't say anything for a long time. In some ways I was hurt by that, but I also understood.

'Gary had similar experiences. However, while we were at the Royal Brompton Hospital we had a letter from someone who has a great deal to cope with in her own life. It was wonderful to know she had time for us.

'I needed people other than my parents and Gary to talk to. I found it quite difficult during the first few weeks, because we had to be isolated. And the people I wanted to come and visit me weren't always the people who came.'

Yet Deb and Gary were on the receiving end of many acts of kindness. 'People knocked on my door with ready-made meals, and one Christian friend did all my washing and ironing for four months.

'Gary and I had a strong relationship, right from the beginning, and all that has happened has strengthened our marriage.'

'They asked me if he was going to die'

At the time of Jacob's illness, Megan and Olivia were aged just four-and-a-half and three. 'The thing they remember most is that Mummy cried when she told them Jacob was poorly. I felt we needed to explain to them what was going on, but I didn't want to frighten them by telling them too much.

'I prayed they would cope and they were absolutely fantastic. Once Jacob was taken off the life-support machine, my mum and dad brought them to the hospital. They stood there and chatted to Jacob as if he was lying in his pram at home. Of course, they asked what all the tubes were.

'I always believed in being completely honest but not to the point of frightening them. So when they asked me if he was going to die, I said I didn't know.

'I don't know how aware they were of death, but Gary's mother had died when I was expecting Megan and we talk about her all the time. They know she's gone to heaven.

'Megan and Olivia have been amazingly patient with Jacob, and with me. All Megan wanted to do when Jacob was ill was to sit and cuddle him. I didn't want to be over-protective. I've tried very hard not to treat Jacob differently. That wouldn't be fair on the girls.'

'They love going'

'Megan and Olivia love going to church and feel terribly deprived if they miss it. They go because they want to and not because I drag them along every Sunday morning. They have quite a strong group of Christian friends already, which I never had as a child.'

And Jacob is there too.

The family attend the church plant from St Mary's, which meets in a local middle school. 'For the first third of the service, we all meet together – adults, children and babies. Children sit with their parents. I feel quite strongly that I want all my children to be part of the service. Jacob loves the songs and sings through the prayers. I feel very relaxed with the children in church, and when *you* feel relaxed the children relax too.

'A third of the way through, the babies go into the crèche and the children go into their different groups. Once a month we have Family Communion.'

A lot else goes on for church families. The week I interviewed Deb, they were due to have an anti-Halloween party. 'We have had big discussions this week with the children as to why they shouldn't go to a Halloween party.' And the church not only has adult home-groups but also a children's one for 7–10s – under adult guidance, 'but it was the children who took the initiative in setting it up.'

'My ultimate ambition…'

Deb is child-minder to three children who also go to the church. 'They are lovely children and they get on well with mine – they are similar in age. I have them about three to four days each week.

'I taught under-sevens in the Sunday school at church for years and years, and I loved that. I run a parents-and-toddlers group every Tuesday morning. Probably three-quarters of the parents who come to that don't go to church. We have a lot of opportunity to discuss parental problems. We have a parents-and toddlers service every three or four months, and some people have started coming to church through that. My ultimate ambition is to start a Christian-based nursery for preschool children.'

On the carpet in front of us, Jacob begins to play with a toy vacuum cleaner.

'Every time I look at my children,' says Deb, 'I'm reminded of how great God is.'

Chapter 7

'DAD, DAD, CAN I GO?'

Raphael remembers very clearly the night of the riots in Lozells in the early 1980s. Shops were being looted and set on fire, and it was all happening not very far from the Birmingham suburb where Raphael and his family live.

'I was going to work. I always left the house just after ten o'clock when I had listened to the headlines on the news. That night there was something about riots in Lozells. When he heard, our son said, "Dad, Dad, can I go?" He wanted to see what was going on.' It was all very different from the world Raphael had known in Jamaica.

He, his sisters and his brothers grew up in Clarendon, about fifty miles from the capital city of Kingston. Raphael's mother still lives in Jamaica but the family has since scattered – some to America, some to Canada and some to England.

Raphael and his brothers and sisters went to Sunday School regularly. Every week, like many children in Britain, they had to memorise a verse of the Bible, to be recited the following Sunday. Now, many years later, Raphael still experiences a thrill of recognition when he comes across verses from those early days.

Following the trade Jesus had followed

His father was employed by the Public Works Department, helping to maintain the roads and doing some agricultural work as well. Raphael himself might have become a tailor, but when he left school those who advised him about his career didn't think he would cope with the precise measurements needed to ensure that jackets are exactly the right fit.

So, somewhat illogically, he was advised to become a carpenter. He served his apprenticeship and showed himself well able to cope with the precise measurements on plans and blueprints! But he also had the satisfaction of knowing he was following the trade Jesus had followed in Joseph's workshop in Nazareth long ago.

Back in the 1950s, people throughout the Caribbean were being encouraged to emigrate. Many thousands left their island homes in search of work and hoped-for prosperity overseas.

'The people here wouldn't accept you'

Raphael's first venture out of the Caribbean was to America on a nine months' contract. That was a culture shock. But, he says, 'I was glad I went there and had experience of that part of the world.'

There is one incident he will never forget. 'I was in Florida, and I was seeking out a church to go to. It was a Friday night. I found a church and met a lady there and asked if I could see the minister. So the minister came to talk to me. I explained that I wanted to worship there, that I was a member of their denomination in Jamaica. "I'm sorry," he said, "but the people here wouldn't accept you because of your colour." He pointed me to another part of the town, a long distance away, where coloured people lived and I would find a church to worship in.

'I was very, very disappointed. It worried me particularly because ministers used to come to Jamaica from America to preach to us and to encourage us.'

Raphael finished his contract and returned home. It was

then that he went to his minister and asked to be baptised. He became a church member and fully committed his life to Christ.

First impressions of England

There was little work for him in Jamaica but apparently a great need for carpenters in England. So, in the early 1960s, boom years for the British building trade, he left the sunshine of the West Indies, crossed the Atlantic and came to Birmingham where one of his sisters was already living. After all, Raphael says, 'anywhere I go, I can serve the Lord Jesus Christ.'

What were his first impressions of England? He laughed. 'Very dull, very grey. Not very encouraging, with the coldness and the short days and long nights. But then you see, I came in November!'

His sister welcomed him warmly and gave him a room. 'I got a job and I coped.' And Raphael quickly found a house-church where he was able to worship.

His bad experience in America wasn't repeated in England. 'At least not in church. But I do remember once at work, when there was a vacancy for a charge-hand, I said to one of my friends, "I'm going to apply for that job." My mate went and told our supervisor and he said, "Over my dead body!"

'You could be prevented from getting ahead because of your colour.'

'Our Lord Jesus was despised and rejected'

'At times like these, my Christian faith has helped me a lot. I remember that our Lord Jesus was despised and rejected, and I remember what happened to his followers in those days.

'Another time one of my workmates brought some leaflets about coloured people into the factory and gave one to our supervisor. I told him that if he distributed any more of those leaflets, I would put in a complaint about him. He stopped, and surprisingly he and I became the best of friends. He lives in Devon now, and I've been down there to see him since I retired. His wife is a Christian and we've discussed the Christian pathway a lot.'

Raphael and his wife had grown up in a same district in Jamaica and had been pupils at the same elementary school. They kept in touch when Raphael was in America. Distance certainly proved no barrier to the development of their relationship, because his wife-to-be was in Cuba when Raphael first came to Britain. She followed him here, and they were married, more than thirty years ago.

They have three grown-up children, two sons and a daughter, who are all still at home. They are obviously well looked after. Their mother comments cryptically, 'I don't give them fish and chips!'

Never allowed to roam the streets

'As parents,' Raphael says modestly, 'we have tried to do what we can. I have never really allowed my wife to go out to work – she has stayed at home to take care of the children.'

He has never forgotten his own upbringing and has followed the example of his parents. 'My mother and father never allowed me to roam the streets or do anything out-of-the-ordinary on a Sunday. We've always encouraged our children to attend church, just as my parents encouraged me. They still go, and our younger son teaches in Sunday School.'

At one stage, Raphael and the family used to attend a place of worship where the sermons were very long and the pews uncomfortably hard. One morning, when their elder son was quite small, he got out of their pew in the middle of the sermon, went to the cloakroom and picked up his coat as if to say, *I've had enough!*

Not long after this, Raphael's wife was ill, and a friend called and asked if she could take their son to her church. Raphael had no objection, so off the boy went to this friend's Sunday School. 'He came back and said, "Daddy, I like that church!" – and he's been going there now for twenty years! We all followed suit, as a family!'

Raphael is an honoured and valued deacon at the church. He also helps in a church project, to keep young people in the area off the streets by teaching them skills such as printing and photography.

Did the children ever rebel against their parents' faith and way of life when they were teenagers? 'No,' says Raphael. 'I remember that whenever our elder son wanted to go out somewhere and I said no, he would start to bite his fingernails and shake his legs. I would know he wasn't happy. But he didn't rebel.'

The night of the riots

The night of the riots was a tragic night in the story of Lozells. It was also a significant night for Raphael's family.

'Our son said, "Dad, Dad, can I go?" I said to him firmly, "I'm going to work now, but if I hear that you've been out of this house tonight…" And he just turned back. Praise the Lord, I was glad. I thank God he didn't disobey me.

'After the riots, they were doing a house-to-house search to find stolen property, and a policeman came down here and knocked on our door to find out what we knew about the fire and the looting. People who had just been passing through Lozells on the night of the riots were caught up in it, and there were arrests. If my son hadn't obeyed me that night, he could have been arrested and might not have a job now.'

It was a special moment of a different kind for the family when their younger son was awarded his university degree and they attended his graduation ceremony.

'Try as nearly as possible to follow God's word'

Raphael and his wife have been married for more than thirty years. If Raphael could give just one piece of advice to a Christian couple getting married, what would it be?

'I think you've got to try as nearly as possible to follow God's word. You have got to dedicate yourselves, as the scripture says, "to training up your children in the way they should go. Then, when they are older, they will not depart from it".'

A framed map of the sunshine island of Jamaica still hangs above the mantelpiece in Raphael's Birmingham home. On the map two Jamaican flags fly proudly, and underneath it is a great cluster of family photographs.

The sun still shines very spasmodically in Birmingham. Raphael and his wife have not been able to transplant the sunshine of the Caribbean into the English Midlands. But they seem successfully to have transplanted the style of Christian family life they both knew when they were youngsters back in Jamaica.

Chapter 8

SEVEN GRANDCHILDREN
AND A TELEPHONE

'How old are your grandchildren?'

Jonathan pulled his electronic organiser out of his pocket. Rosemary began to tell me their names and ages, while he pressed a button or two to check on birthday dates and make sure his wife was correct.

It was in a distant, pre-electronic age that today's grandparents went to school. When Rosemary saw Jonathan for the first time, fifty-odd years ago, he was in his school swimming pool, breaking the one-length record. But other events at school had an even more decisive influence on their lives...

Rosemary grew up in a South London suburb. She remembers the delights of playing in a garden when, around the time she was three, the family moved from a flat to a house. She remembers how interested she was as a five-year-old in the preparations for the birth of her brother. They were a typical suburban family. They didn't go to church very much but Rosemary went to the occasional children's service.

'On the whole I enjoyed secondary school. Geography was my best subject, and I liked hockey. I played left back. The link was my hockey coach – she was a Welsh international and she also taught geography. She was a very good teacher.

'I was confirmed because my best friend was confirmed

and for no other reason, though my mother thought it was a good idea too. I was thoroughly confused by the confirmation classes. I tried asking questions but I never felt satisfied with the answers I got.

'Sometimes seniors from four girls' secondary schools in our area met together to discuss the Christian faith.'

'I'd been looking for God'

It so happened that the headmistress from one of these four schools, who was a Christian, knew the Rev Bryan Green, a leading evangelist in the 1930s. So at Christmas time 1938, a Christmas overshadowed (at least for adults) by the abdication of Edward VIII, she invited Bryan Green to speak at a carol service for the girls from all four schools. It was held in a local church. Rosemary remembers the service well.

'It was terribly informal. Bryan Green didn't look a bit like a parson. He was a very good communicator and it was really easy to listen to him. His text was John 14:6, where Jesus says, "I am the way and the truth and the life. No one comes to the Father except through me."

'This was just the revelation I needed. I'd been looking for God in those discussions at school, and that verse showed me I had to come to God through Jesus.'

Bible studies and a camp

'Two girls from a form above me at school, who also played hockey, went to a local Bible class for fourteen-year-olds and over. These girls would call for me every Sunday afternoon. They would cycle over to my house and then walk with me to the Bible class – my mother wouldn't let me cycle on a Sunday.

'The class ran mid-week Bible studies, and I was encouraged to start reading the Bible with the help of Scripture Union's *Daily Bread*. We also had a Whitsun camp under canvas – no problem to me, I'd been a Girl Guide!

'The second year I went to the camp, the padre was Harold Ling who was on the Scripture Union staff. He led the beach mission at Perranporth in Cornwall every summer. That's how I became involved in beach missions. I was a member of the Perranporth team for two years before joining the Women's Royal Naval Service.

'I had taken my School Certificate (the equivalent of GCSE) in the summer of 1939. Rather than be evacuated from London with the rest of the school when war broke out, I left and taught myself to type. I went to work for a leading publishing firm before becoming a meteorologist in the Wrens.'

Jonathan remembers how he and his brother were taken to sail their toy boats on the pond at Hampstead Heath on Sunday afternoons, after they had been to Sunday School. The family occupied what was 'almost a family pew' in a large Baptist church in North London. His father, who was a ship's chandler by trade, edited the church magazine. It was a great adventure for Jonathan and his brother when their father took them to Euston station to send the magazine on its way to be printed.

But this adventure was not to continue. Jonathan's father had served in the Royal Navy in the First World War, and during that time he had contracted rheumatic fever which left its mark on his heart. When he was in his mid-forties and Jonathan was only ten years old, he had a brief attack of influenza and, as a result of his weakened heart, he died.

Jonathan's widowed mother moved the family south of the Thames to be near her brother, a leading barrister and defence lawyer. 'He was very kind to us,' Jonathan recalls. What's more, his uncle was a governor of an independent day-school and he arranged for his nephews to go there on very reasonable terms. His mother sent Jonathan to a local Crusaders class – his father had been one of the very first

Crusaders – and he found this class a tremendous help.

Rosemary's brother went to the same day-school, and this is how she found herself by the side of the swimming pool when Jonathan broke the one-length record.

'I had no idea I needed to do anything about sin'

Jonathan's school was one of the very few at the time to have a Christian Union.

'It was at the school CU that I came to the Lord. I believe the speaker that day came from the London City Mission – I seem to remember that he was a missionary to taxi-drivers. He used Naaman as an example of sin. I'd been to Crusaders but I had no idea I needed to do anything about sin. That was when I made my decision to come to Christ. I was fourteen.'

War came, and four years later Jonathan, the star swimmer, tried to join the Navy. But they wouldn't have him because he is colour-blind, so he went straight from school to university.

In the same church

During the war Rosemary went 'church-hunting', trying to find a church where she felt 'comfortable'. One evening she attended a Baptist church. She was attracted to the preaching, but what impressed her most was that, at the end of the service, a girl of about her own age introduced herself, took the trouble to walk all the way home with Rosemary and then bussed back. 'I was so impressed that I went to the church again, and again...' It was there that she met up once more with Jonathan.

In the immediate post-war years the church enjoyed a boom time. There were well over a hundred people, with ages ranging from four to fourteen, at Young Worshippers every Sunday morning – Rosemary was one of the leaders – and there was a Young Christians' Training Class every

Friday night. Though the title now sounds clumsy and archaic, it was to prove a strategic venture. Meanwhile, Jonathan, Rosemary and many others helped out at children's Bible rallies in a less respectable suburb a few miles away.

Jonathan proposed to Rosemary in the grounds of Polesden Lacey, a stately home in Surrey. After they were married, they moved to the Midlands and continued to work amongst children in a local Sunday School. They helped to found three new Crusader classes and continued to be involved with Crusaders as their family grew up.

Family get-together for fifteen

Jonathan and Rosemary now have four grown-up sons, three daughters-in-law ('They're marvellous!') and seven grandchildren, all of whose birth dates are, of course, faithfully recorded on Jonathan's electronic organiser. Every year, around Christmas, they all meet at Jonathan and Rosemary's home for a great family get-together.

Jonathan has retired from his academic appointment, and he and Rosemary now attend the Methodist church in the village where they live. They are, of course, no longer the standard family. So do they feel at all left out at Family Services?

'No,' says Rosemary, 'because I relate "Family Services" not to the natural family but to the church family, where you can be a hundred years or three months old. I've never thought of them in any other way.'

Most of the leaders in her local church share this view, though they are aware there are some people who aren't married who feel a bit out of it. 'This is why we try to promote the idea of the church family. The big thing is to get as many people as possible to take part, people of all ages. Sometimes they come out of a Family Service saying, "That was a nice children's service", and I feel a bit narked.'

Neither of them feels that grandparents should just sit on the sidelines and watch. 'I don't think you should desert young people's work,' Jonathan comments, 'unless there is somebody, preferably better than yourself, to take over.' No doubt remembering that Young Christians' Training Class long ago, he adds, 'Ideally, what ought to happen is for younger people to be trained to take our places. But if there's no one available, we should carry on and try to keep ourselves up-to-date.'

Even if the phone bills rocket

Jonathan and Rosemary find the telephone vital in helping them to contribute to their grandchildren's spiritual development. 'One of the big things we can do is to pray for them. And when you keep in touch with what they're doing, that helps you to pray' – though the phone bills may rocket at times.

They are thrilled that their thirteen-year-old grandson so obviously enjoyed the responsibility he was given at a Christian camp for younger children. They are equally thrilled when their younger granddaughters bring them paintings to adorn the walls of their kitchen and tell them, 'We've done these specially for you!'

Rosemary says, 'I'm encouraged by our grandchildren's attitude towards us. I never get the impression that they think we're old. I often go down to the rec with them, where there's an assault course!'

Looking back

When they reflect on their days as parents, Rosemary and Jonathan are thankful that they approached some issues in the way they did. 'There's one tricky point,' says Rosemary, 'that I feel strongly about. I was practically always in when the children came home from school. If ever I was going to be out, I would leave a note. One day I forgot, so I was left a note: "Mummy, you forgot to leave me a note. Where are you?"

'And we always welcomed our children's friends, so we knew who their friends were.'

Jonathan and Rosemary are thankful that their sons went to Crusader camps and that, as a family, they spent summer holidays at Scripture Union missions. 'Beach missions helped enormously. There were leaders in their twenties telling them exactly the same truths that we told them the rest of the year.'

But that wasn't the only significant thing about those holidays: also important was the fun, the silly things they did, and the fact that the team spent time with the children.

Regrets and hopes

Two of their sons are vigorously active in Christian service. Their greatest regret is that another son has been disabled from birth. He suffers from cerebral palsy and is deaf. 'We have prayed again and again, and taken him to people with gifts of healing. But somehow the Lord hasn't completely healed him yet.

'To ask why this should be is a natural reaction. You feel there must be a purpose in it, though we won't know what that is this side of heaven.'

Rosemary and Jonathan looked after their disabled son full-time until he was eight, then he went to special schools. Now he lives away from home, though he comes back to stay with his parents from time to time.

How did his disability affect his brothers? 'They were wonderful at helping him walk. The experts told us he would never walk, and he didn't until he was five. But his older brothers used to stand him up against a wall and put their hands out to him to stop him falling. Then they would gradually move further and further away, encouraging him all the while to take a few steps forward.'

And now the next generation just accept him. 'Our grandchildren talk naturally about their uncle, and he always joins us at our Christmas family get-together.'

Jonathan and Rosemary just enjoy life. There is so much to do. They don't think a lot about what might happen if they get to be eighty or ninety. 'But if we're still here, it would be great to have great-grandchildren.'

They have two final pieces of advice to offer new Christian grandparents. 'Don't tell your children how to bring up your grandchildren. And make sure you love your daughters- and sons-in-law as much as you love your own children.'

Chapter 9

WELCOMED WITH LOVE

I know most people don't like airports but I confess that I do. I still find it exciting to see the names of romantic far-away places on the board in the departure lounge, to mingle with the cosmopolitan crowds, and watch the greetings and farewells.

It was at Luton Airport that Mick first set eyes on Karen, not as a fellow passenger but behind the scenes as one of his colleagues in the security department. It was some months before they got together. Both of them were carrying around a lot of baggage.

'A bit of a tearaway'

When Mick left school, he followed in his father's footsteps and went to work at the brickyard, in the wages office. However, after a couple of years he was made redundant – the company had to halve their workforce.

Mick had a second spell at the brickyard when trade recovered. But, as he explains, 'It was a bit of a dead-end job and I was something of a tearaway. I thought I needed some discipline in my life.

'We packed up work at 12.30 on Fridays at the brick-yard, and I usually went off to Bedford for the afternoon. One Friday, I looked in at the Careers Information Office and they told me about the RAF Regiment. Within a week I was well on the way to joining up.'

Mick served in Hong Kong and Northern Ireland, and then spent two and a half years in Germany. While he was in the RAF, he took up the guitar – it was 'a ticket to free beer'! More significantly, 'I found that it was a way of communicating with people.' Mick didn't rate himself as a fluent talker.

Not long after he left the RAF, he took a job on the security staff at Luton Airport. He has been there now for twenty years. 'I started as a patrolman and worked my way up the ladder.'

He married. His wife had three children from her previous marriage, and in due course Mick started to go with his stepsons to a parade service at an Anglican church in Luton. 'I soon decided I wanted to know more. I joined a ten-week instruction course, and I was confirmed. However, it didn't mean much to me at the time.'

'It surprised me that Jesus is God'

'I always believed there was God. I always believed there was Jesus. But how the two related to each other I didn't know. It surprised me that Jesus is actually God.

'I needed more than the ten-week course. It wasn't until two years later that I actually became a Christian at a renewal weekend at Letchworth. That was when I was first filled with the Spirit.'

As a new Christian, Mick began to use his musical gift. He started to play in a house-group, and two or three years later he was invited to play at the worship services. The church already had one worship band, but 'as we had services at 9.15 and 11, I was invited to form another. Soon I was playing on three Sundays out of four. On the fourth Sunday I worked at the airport.'

Although the congregation were used to more traditional forms of music, they responded well to the band Mick was leading. 'But this is where things started going wrong. I was playing my guitar for all the wrong reasons. I began to do it for the recognition. I used to get all puffed up. I actually stopped playing for a while.

'I was also on the PCC, but I soon faded into the background and eventually left because of what was happening in my private life.'

Mick's marriage lasted until 1990. 'It broke down for many reasons. I tried to hold it together and I was prepared to work at the relationship. But it fell apart. The children were growing up, and it had been the children rather than my ex-wife who had cemented the relationship.

'One day, at the end of 1991, I was looking out of my office and I thought to myself, *That's a nice young lady.* Karen had joined the security staff at Luton Airport. I was one of the duty officers but we were on different crews. It was some months before we got together.'

Karen had been born and bred in Hemel Hempstead. When she left school, she worked for a firm of bookbinders. Shortly afterwards she became pregnant and married the father of her child.

'My husband had no faith of any sort but I've always had an interest in things spiritual. I started going to clairvoyants and to spiritualist churches. I was seeking something. I didn't know what.

'We had another daughter the following year, in 1978. Our marriage lasted till 1990. My husband was quite a violent person, particularly after a drink. He never had time for the children. I stuck to the relationship, but when I got the job at the airport I decided it was time to make a break. It was the best thing I've ever done.'

She first noticed Mick at a Christmas 'do'. 'But I didn't notice him as soon as he noticed me!'

'I was the one who was lost'
When she and Mick began to get together, what bothered

Karen was the frequency with which Mick would go and see Bob Gunn, the airport chaplain. 'I used to think Bob was trying to talk Mick out of having any sort of relationship with me.'

In fact, Mick had known the chaplain for many years. 'He used to be my vicar. We were great friends. I used to talk to him about everything.' And their conversations at this stage weren't quite as Karen imagined.

Mick says, 'I'd turned my back on the Lord but I knew he hadn't turned his back on me. There were little things along the way that made me realise I hadn't lost him. *I* was the one who was lost.'

His turmoil deepened when he met Karen. 'I started to realise I could have Jesus in my life without Karen, but I couldn't have Karen in my life without Jesus. This was causing me terrible problems. I was so cut up. I desperately wanted the Lord's company again, and Bob was trying desperately to get through to me that God was a God of love and forgiveness. Because I'd ended a marriage...'

'At her wits' end'

'Bob would go through the scriptures with me. I believed the only way I could get back to the Lord was to stop seeing Karen. I was very mixed up inside. Karen didn't understand what was going on in my head. She was at her wits' end. It must have been terrible for her.'

Mick and Karen were living together and, in his turmoil, Mick was looking for somewhere to worship. They went to a carol service together at South Hill Church in Hemel Hempstead. 'The people at the church were tremendous, right from the moment we walked in through the door. They were so friendly.'

'Nobody pointed the finger,' says Karen. 'Nobody condemned us. They accepted us just as we were.'

And God started to move.

I wouldn't have missed that night for anything'

Karen's daughter Tina had already started going to the youth club at South Hill Church. 'She became quite involved, went off to Spring Harvest and became a Christian. I had a mixed reaction to that. I was a bit concerned, but I saw the change in her. She had been a bit of a rebel.

'She encouraged me to go and hear the evangelist Luis Palau. Mick took me, and at the end of the meeting they gave us an opportunity to go forward to a room at the back. I can remember this woman praying for me. It was like having a sensation welling up inside me. It was just like the birth of a newborn baby. Mick was there.'

Mick says, 'I wouldn't have missed that night for anything.

'A few weeks later, Karen's elder daughter Julie became a Christian. It was incredible the way the Lord was working. The whole family had been saved, and I thought, *If God loves them enough to draw them to himself, he must still love me.*

'At that stage, I was living in Luton on my own. I felt that for us to go on living together would be a stumbling-block to my faith, but for us to live apart would be a stumbling-block to our relationship. But I started to feel that my faith was right and our relationship was right.

'One day I told Karen that we should buy a house. She agreed.

'Houses that were ideal fell through. But as soon as one door shut, another one opened. The Lord was really good to us. Eventually, within minutes of a house we wanted being taken off the market, we were offered this one. It was the right size, the area was OK and another couple from our church live down the road. Things were falling into place. God wouldn't have blessed us if he didn't want us to be here.'

On the day he had proposed buying the house, Mick had

also asked Karen to marry him. Karen had said yes to both proposals, and she and Mick were married in April 1995.

In their marriage preparation talks, Brian, their pastor, 'took us to the heart of Jesus. He showed us that we were forgiven, that God still loved us for what we were and was showing he loved us by the way he had taken care of our whole situation. All our doubts vanished and we both knew we faced a wonderful future together, he had blessed us so much. And now he's giving us a child. So it's going on and on.'

A home full of love

Mick and Karen chose not to know the sex of their child before the birth and, with just a couple of weeks to go, they were full of hopes for their baby. 'I hope we can bring him or her up in a Christian home full of love,' says Mick. 'I nearly lost my way. I wouldn't want that to happen again.'

A cell group from their church now meets in their home, of which they are the hosts. The house has a sizeable living room, though if all the twenty-eight people who could attend the group actually did so on the same evening, it could be a bit of a crush...

'We worship, pray and study the Bible together, and we natter.' And do they sing? 'Oh, yes!' It didn't take long for the church to notice Mick knew all the worship songs. 'For three or four weeks in 1994 a lot of musicians were away, so we put together a makeshift band to lead the worship.' Now Mick is a regular member of the worship team.

When Mick and Karen first arrived at their church, they were living together. Their advice to Christians meeting couples in a similar situation who come through the church doors is clear: 'Welcome them, greet them with love and with a listening ear. Leave the talking until later.'

Chapter 10

FROM CHURCHGOING TO FAITH

Jim and Mary have lived all their lives in the Black Country, that part of Britain which owes its name to the soot and grime of the Industrial Revolution. Today the physical blackness has gone but the name lives on as a reminder of a history of honest toil in grim conditions, often for a meagre wage.

The psychological legacy lives on too. Even today, many Black Country people lack self-confidence – or maybe they have more humility as a result of this legacy! In this respect Jim and Mary would appear to be atypical, but they say it's only because they have recognised this inherent character trait and have tried to overcome it.

Nor do they live in a typical Black Country home. Theirs is a large, friendly, rambling house with a long and unusual history. Wooden beams form the ceiling of a sizeable entrance hall which has welcomingly comfortable chairs and an elegant grandfather clock.

The Black Country tradition is to stay near your parents, and there Jim and Mary certainly are typical. Mary moved no less than six miles when she married Jim and that, as she says, 'is a long way for a Black Country person!'

But Jim has always lived in the very same road. He began life in the house where he and his family live now. When he was about three, his father, who was a builder, built another house – just four doors away.

Since he and Mary were married, they have lived in four houses in the same road. 'We're very adventurous in our choice of location!'

Both Jim and Mary have been churchgoers since childhood, and they have had quite a range of church experiences.

'Always made to go to Sunday School'

Mary and her family lived in a terraced house, and at the bottom of the garden there was a communal strip of land. One of her earliest memories is of playing mud pies there with a little girl whose house also backed onto the strip.

She and her brother were always made to go to Sunday School at the Methodist church opposite where they lived. 'I quite liked it. But on Sunday evenings my parents used to go to the Anglican church where they'd been married. I have memories of polo mints and dark churches, and that's why I still don't like evening services!'

Mary reckons she came to faith in Christ gradually over a long period of time, 'in fits and starts'. 'A major turning point was when I was in my teens. We had one or two very good teachers in the youth section at the Methodist church, who were very challenging. But when I got to about eighteen and started courting, a lot of the churchgoing dropped off.'

When Mary left school, she did a two-year course to become a qualified nursery nurse. She then worked with young children, initially at a nursery unit attached to a school in Tipton, a Black Country town noted for its own dialect. Tipton is rumoured to have its own language. According to Mary, there are certainly local variations on standard English words. Until recently, some of the older folk still used in everyday speech the 'thees' and 'thous' you find in the King James Bible.

Mary was nearly eighteen when she met Jim. 'We went

out for about six months and then split up. But after another nine months we got back together again, and we've been together ever since!'

'Jesus was the only one who had died for me'

'I was confirmed,' Mary recalls, 'when I was twenty-six, but I don't think Jesus came into my life until about six years ago. That was at a Scripture Union training weekend at Swanwick. I went because I was involved with the children in Sunday School. I realised I needed to do more to make the teaching relevant to them. I didn't want to teach in Sunday School the way I had been taught. I wanted knowing about Jesus to be exciting.

'Swanwick is in Derbyshire, and I'd never driven as far as that in my life before. And we drove there on a dark November night!

'The whole weekend was an amazing experience, and it was there that the full impact of knowing Jesus really hit me. During the worship we sang the chorus, "You laid aside your majesty", and I realised Jesus was the only one who had died for me. I came home full of enthusiasm, and I couldn't sleep that night.'

Dreary practices

'I was a spoilt only child,' confesses Jim. 'Ours was a nominally Christian family. I used to go to Sunday School in a nonconformist church on a Sunday morning. It rather miffed me that you could only get enough stars in your book to get a prize if you went both in the morning *and* in the afternoon.

'They had a typical staged Sunday School Anniversary, when you had to wear white or whatever the colour scheme was. And if you didn't have any clothes of the right colour, you didn't get on the stage.

'After weeks and weeks of dreary practices, where you

had to learn all the songs off by heart, all your relations came. It was usually in the summertime and sweltering hot. If you were a star pupil, you might get to recite a bit of poetry.

'When I was about seven, I was asked to join an Anglican choir. That was OK. However, though the choirmaster was kind-hearted, he was very strict and interested in getting things right. We were paid at the rate of three old pennies per Sunday, but to get your money you had to turn up to mid-week practices – and Wednesday night practices in a cold church were appalling. They went on and on. It was worse than being at school. But I stuck it until I was about twelve.

'I did get confirmed, and I lasted about another couple of years in that church. Then I stopped until Mary and I started going to church together. I had a faith of sorts but I certainly wasn't a Christian.'

Money and brass

'After we got married, Mary and I joined an Anglican church which we went to very regularly for more than twenty years. But I didn't go on Sunday mornings because I played in a brass band that took part in various competitions. As a band we did the equivalent in football terms of starting in the fourth division and getting right up to the Premiership. Playing in the band started out as a hobby, but it gradually became a bit more than that, so I packed it in after about twenty-one years.

'I used to go to church on Sunday evenings and also to the 8 o'clock morning communion service. I served on the PCC, and then was churchwarden for a few years. But I know I wasn't a Christian then.

'It was the kind of church where everything revolved around finances, and this was a turn-off for me. I'm a chartered accountant and I believe we're called to be good stewards of money, but we're not called to make it a god. There was row after row on this PCC – it was appalling. But I thought this was just church life.

'Mary and a friend built up the Sunday School from just a handful of children to around thirty-five. We took them to adventure camps several years running. The church also ran children's holiday clubs in the summer, based on Scripture Union materials. The vicar's wife, who is still a very good friend of ours, used to be the leader. We would have as many as a hundred children at these holiday clubs. And all we would get at the end from the PCC would be remarks like "They're not paying for the water they use!"

'In the end I moved to another church. Mary still had to fulfil some commitments, but she too changed too after about six months. We had moved further along the path than the church we had been attending was prepared to go. So we went to a much more evangelical church, and that's where I became a Christian. I've been there nearly five years now.'

God's sense of humour

'I said I'd never go on a PCC or get involved in church finances again, but God has a sense of humour and I'm now church treasurer! At our present church we run our finances very differently from our previous one. We try to see what God's will is, then we go for it. The money has always followed.

'The church is made up largely of single-parent families. Most people are on supplementary benefit from the Department of Social Security. The wages in our area are appalling. Despite that, giving per family is phenomenal. We give away more than a third of our income, and it seems the more you give away, the more God honours that and the more the money comes in.'

Always getting up to mischief

Jim and Mary have two sons who are now both teenagers. Like their parents, they went to church from an early age and grew up with church being part of life. Their elder son Daniel says, 'When I was younger, I quite liked going. But when I was about thirteen, there were some Sundays when I didn't want to go. I remember we did once have a bit of a confab on the landing about it. I was made to go that time.

'But, to be honest, I suppose we liked it because there were a group of us and we used to have some fun. We were always getting up to some sort of mischief.

'Once we made what was a broom closet into an Egyptian palace. We spent weeks constructing it, and we used toilet rolls to wrap people up as mummies. At the end, we burnt all the rubbish in the church car park. When the fire was almost out, an elderly lady came along. She was furious. She said the car park had exploded!'

And when he was about four, at a Christingle service, Daniel succeeded in setting light to his service sheet by skilful use of one of the candles. 'Oh, look! It's on fire!' he said excitedly. But this attempt at ecclesiastical arson progressed no further – they managed to put out the flames.

'A bit of a wild year'

Daniel committed his life to Christ at the Scripture Union camp at Salcombe, Devon. 'I was sixteen and had just left school, having finished my exams. I'd had a bit of a wild year really and was going down the slippery slope somewhat.

'I did quite a lot to get out of going on that camp. I went and got a job at the local DSS office. But Mum and Dad had paid for the holiday, so I thought I'd better go to stop them moaning. I thought I would do the rock-climbing and when it came to the Christian bits I'd just sit there.

'I went on the advance party. I was with two other lads

who weren't Christians, and we went down the town and had a few drinks and did some other things we shouldn't have.

'I suppose I thought I was a Christian but I came fast to the realisation that I wasn't. It got me thinking and I said to whoever was out there, "Show me a sign, or else I'll forget it and carry on the way I am."

'I was sitting in the service one night, listening to a talk. There was a big snow picture on the wall. The guy who had developed this picture had discovered that you could see the face of Christ in it, though we didn't know this at the time. I was sitting there, and I saw Christ's face. The Holy Spirit came down and I became a Christian. I know, though, that I'm not perfect by any means.

'I'm quite glad I was made to go to church. It gave me a good basis and I've made a lot of friends there too.'

'I feel I missed out a bit not seeing Dad'

Mary has found being a parent difficult at times but on the whole has enjoyed it. 'I suppose my nursery training helped.

'Looking back now, I'm sorry Jim and I spent so much of our time renovating houses. This is our third house. We put a twenty-foot extension onto our second house – Jim built it himself with the help of our parents and in-laws. Daniel was climbing up ladders when he was eighteen months old! But all this, and the social entertaining we used to do as part of Jim's career, gave us less time for the family.

'We did try to do things together. We took picnics to Jim's brass band concerts and tried to make them family times, and we've always gone on family holidays in our caravan.'

Though he did miss not seeing his dad as much as he could have done, Daniel gives his parents quite high marks for the way they brought him up. 'You can't *make* your children become Christians. Sometimes the more you try to push them into it, the more they move away. The ultimate goal is for them to become Christians, but it doesn't always happen.'

View from the magistrates' bench

Mary is a Justice of the Peace. Sitting on the local magistrates' bench, she inevitably sees people from all kinds of families. 'I just thank God for my family and for the way we are together when I see the mess that so many youngsters are making of their lives. So many kids have no role models. They're left to do their own thing, and many of them are just put out on the streets until it's time for bed.'

Jim and Mary's advice to Christian couples is, 'Always keep communication open and say exactly what's going on. Don't let things build up, keeping the lid on until they boil over with anger and resentment. Start the marriage off truthfully, and just keep working at it all the time. And don't let the sun go down on your anger.'

'Our sons must do what they want to do'

Jim retired nearly five years ago. He had always said it was his ambition to retire at forty and he nearly achieved that. 'I'd seen a number of my colleagues die at around forty-five. I didn't want to spend the rest of my life in the fast lane of the rat race. My retirement has given us time to be together as a family and to decide the things we want to do. We still entertain as much as we used to, but not out of any sense of obligation.'

Jim still looks after a few clients who are also personal friends, and he works every bit as hard voluntarily as most people do for a salary. But his voluntary work isn't all accountancy: God has been channelling his gifts and considerable energies in new directions. One of his major ventures has been the setting up of a Christian retreat house 'for refreshing, renewal and revival'.

'I work from home and I can choose my hours. It's marvellous! On Monday mornings I pinch myself to make sure that it's real.'

Are Mary and Jim hoping their sons will follow true Black Country tradition and move just down the road? 'No,' they both say firmly. 'The Black Country custom of staying near your parents stops you from having any freedom,' says Mary.

'Our sons must do what they want to do,' says Jim. 'Daniel may end up doing some kind of unconventional church work, and I dare say it might well be overseas!'

Chapter 11

'WE'RE DIFFERENT
BUT WE BELONG TOGETHER'

Malc and Eunice live with their two young sons in an industrial city in the heart of England.

Eunice was brought up as an only child in a very different environment – on a farm on the borders of Devon and Cornwall. Her father was treasurer of the local Methodist chapel, and she was sent to a Methodist boarding school in the West Country.

'I was confirmed at boarding school when I was fifteen. I regarded myself as a Christian at school, and I was sometimes called upon to lead the prayers. But I suppose my faith was rather academic. We had lots of missionaries who used to come and urge us to follow their example. It was a school where you had the opportunity of seeing a lot of people live out their faith.

'Unfortunately, church was sometimes used as a punishment. If we were naughty, we were made to dress up in our Sunday suits, which were horrible anyway, and march down to church – even if there wasn't a service on – and then march back again.

'When I went to Warwick University, seeing how other people lived gradually made me question my faith. At some point during the first term, my head knowledge of the Christian faith turned into heart knowledge. I couldn't say precisely when I became a Christian, but one day I had a vision of a garden, a bright light and a shining figure I believed to be Christ saying, "You are my child. Don't doubt it." '

Not exactly love at first sight

It was at Warwick that Eunice first met Malc. Her initial impressions of him were not very favourable. 'He lived in the next block to us. Two of the girls on my corridor belonged to the Christian Union, and when we went across for our evening meal they would say, "Shall we call for Malc?" I would say, "Do we have to?", because I found him very embarrassing. I had a lot of friends along our corridor, and Malc would come bouncing along, talking about Christianity, and I would just cringe.

'The other memory I have of Malc is of him singing the Gnome song at a Christian Union house-party.

'Some of us, including Malc, used to go to discos as a group, and he and I started going out together half way through our second year.'

Malc was born in Manchester and still proudly calls himself a Mancunian, though his family moved to Cheshire when he was eight. He was number three in a family of five, with two brothers and two sisters. However, his older sister was disabled and died when he was seventeen. Malc says he owes a great deal to the moral values and integrity of his parents. They were a churchgoing family, though his mother found her daughter's disability difficult to cope with.

During Malc's fourth year at secondary school, friends at school asked him to come to the youth group at their church. This group used to go with a lay preacher to other churches in the area, singing and playing their guitars.

'I was just learning to play the guitar and I had no objection to going round singing in churches. At the same time, a teacher started a Christian group at our school. These friends and I went along to that too. I would have called myself a Christian, but I began to realise that what they understood being a Christian meant and what I understood were completely different.'

'Lads of my age reading the Bible every day'

'In my fifth year, a new RE teacher at school took over the Christian Union. In December 1973 I went with him to a Scripture Union New Year Conference at Pateley Bridge. That conference made a huge impact on me. I thought I was doing all the things that Christians should do – I went to church, I read my Bible. I was using Scripture Union's *Daily Bread* at the time, and I read right through the five days' notes before I left for the conference.

'But when I got to Pateley Bridge I was quite stunned. Here were all these lads of my age, in the dormitory, reading the Bible *every* day! I saw it was really important to them.

'I felt there was something wrong in me, and about two weeks later I went to a Christian meeting in Congleton. I can't remember what the speaker said but I saw then that I couldn't just be a hanger-on. That was when I made my real commitment to Christ.' So it was as a committed Christian that Malc went to Warwick University, where he soon met Eunice. While she had found him embarrassing, he at first thought she was 'a bit odd'.

'She was a member of the Christian Union but she would say things that didn't quite tie in with being a Christian. I guess it was simply because she was trying to wind me up, and it probably worked!'

Eunice left university with a degree in law and went on to study for her solicitor's exams. While she was at law school in Chester, Malc spent a year with Community Service Volunteers, working on a project in Nottinghamshire. Then the local council provided a grant so that what he had been doing voluntarily became a paid job, and he stayed on.

'We ought to get married'

'However, when I moved to Nottinghamshire, I wrote to Eunice, breaking off the relationship for all sorts of pious and godly reasons. In fact, I was just scared. I knew the only way this relationship could develop was by us getting married, and the thought of that was frightening!

'But a year later I went over to Chester to see her. We went out together that night, and I told her that I thought we ought to get back together again and if we got back together we ought to get married. And in a moment of weakness she said yes!'

Today Eunice not only shares with Malc in looking after their two sons, nine-year-old Lloyd and seven-year-old Joe: she also works part-time as a solicitor in private practice, dealing with litigation, and she is national chair of the Network of Access and Child Contact Centres. 'There are more than 200 of these centres round the country. I find it a bit frustrating, because there is so much lobbying, fund-raising and training to do and I don't have the time or the resources to do it.'

On neutral ground

Eunice was the coordinator of the Coventry Children's Contact Centre for four years. 'The centre provides a neutral venue where children can meet and play in a controlled environment with the parent they aren't living with. There may have been considerable mistrust between a mum and dad after separation, perhaps because of violence, and the parent who has the child may be reluctant to meet the other on home ground. The centre provides a place where they can leave or collect their child. When they come to the centre, they don't actually have to meet.

'In some families, the concern is whether the visiting parent can really look after the child. But there's no opportunity to drink or inject drugs at the centre, so the child is safe. There are other people around and there are toys and it's warm.

'I remember a young girl – she was only about sixteen or seventeen – who brought her baby to the centre. The dad, who wasn't much older himself, came with his mum. She was a typical large, grandmother figure, and at first the baby's mum was a bit uncertain about her. But after about six weeks Grandma would come with the clothes she had knitted for the baby. And after about twelve weeks the young mum told us Grandma was going to have the baby for the night so she could go out to a disco. She had lost contact with her own parents and realised how much her own child needed a grandparent. She told me how glad she was she had been able to make contact with her ex-partner's mother.'

The Network has international links, and Eunice has visited Australia to lecture on her experiences.

Malc is full-time youth pastor of a large city-centre Baptist church, with responsibility for the children's and young people's activities and for integrating the younger generation into the life of the church. 'It's a challenging role. I have to keep asking how children and young people fit into what we do, how they can participate in our services, how we can be the church family together. I've been here for nine years and I'm still asking those questions. We've found some of the answers but not all of them.'

'Big shock when they started school'

Because Eunice works both inside and outside the home, there is always the tension of wanting to do more things than she can manage. 'Though the children don't need me all the time, I feel guilty when I'm upstairs sorting out correspondence for the Network when they're around.'

Lloyd and Joe are old enough to know about the work their father does in the church. Malc says, 'They've been brought up in an environment where talking about Jesus is normal, and the big shock to them when they started school was that their friends and their friends' parents didn't think that. Lloyd found it very difficult, and the time may come when they find what I do embarrassing.

'But at the moment they're very enthusiastic about getting involved. During church services, Lloyd likes to be in charge of overhead projector acetates. He takes the job very seriously and I think he does it better than almost anyone else in the church!

'Lloyd and Joe are very natural about what they believe. I was talking to Joe recently – like lots of children, he had tried to get out of trouble by denying he was responsible for something that had gone wrong. So I asked him if he wanted to tell the truth. He said that he did but he was scared. I asked him how he was going to stop being scared, and his answer was "I can ask God to help me."

'I sometimes think their expectations when they pray are higher than ours.'

'It's good that the children have role models in church who are younger than we are,' says Eunice, 'and that people who come here to see us also talk about normal things like football.'

Malc adds, 'They want to be part of what's going on. We have a house-group here each week. The first night the group met, Lloyd helped me get the room ready. Then he disappeared and came back five minutes later with his Bible. He wanted to join in. I had to tell him it wasn't really for him, which he accepted. But later he asked when he *would* be able to join in. I told him in about four years' time!'

A broad understanding of family

'Our children have a very broad understanding of family. When Joe was at nursery school, at a parents' evening we were asked, "Apart from yourselves, there are only Lloyd and Joe at home, aren't there?" We said yes. "Oh! Well, he must have got mixed up." It appeared that when they had asked Joe who was in his family, he reeled off a whole long list of names – the names of friends from the church who come to the house a lot. He saw the church as his family and I was very pleased about that.'

What makes a church a real family? 'It's a mixture of friendship between people with common interests, commitment to each other and care for one another when there are problems. Obviously, in a Christian community, prayer also plays an important part.'

'Most of the time,' Malc says, 'I'm thrilled by the church family here. There are lots of good things. Best of all is a willingness to try and work things out together. Sometimes there are sticking points and complaints, particularly about things for all-age groups, but there's a willingness to try and get things right.'

How does he integrate young people into the life of the church, when the older generation have lived through a period of such enormous change? 'By encouraging people at both extremes of the generations to talk to each other and to consider one another. If a young person says a service was boring, or an older person says it was too loud or irreverent, I ask them to consider whether other people might have been blessed by God through it. I try to encourage an attitude that says, "I'm not just here for what I can get. We're here together to help one another. Perhaps at the moment this isn't right for me, but it may be right for somebody else." In return, we in the leadership make a commitment to devise worship with aspects acceptable to all ages. Better to take people with you than to drag them.'

'I realise increasingly as I get older myself that all the things that were fixed points for the older generation – their environment, their city – are changing at an accelerating rate. Perhaps their friends are dying, their health is failing. The one fixed point in their lives is the church they may have belonged to for seventy or eighty years. To find suddenly that change is going on there too is frightening! We have a responsibility not just to foist new ideas on people but to discuss those ideas with them.

'But young people need to be given the opportunity to contribute in services, not only in worship but in other ways. You need to take them seriously.'

Eunice coordinates the Sunday School. On a Sunday morning, 'the children are in what we call young worshippers' groups to begin with. There are five different groups, though two of them combine for a period of worship. At twelve o'clock all the young worshippers go into the church for the last ten or fifteen minutes. Occasionally we have all-age services, where the children will be in the church for the whole time. Sometimes we have split services – one in the usual worship area, which is quieter and more traditional, and the other in the church hall, which is louder and more interactive. Everyone, whatever their age, can choose which they want to go to.' In practice none of the children opts for the more traditional service, whereas a number of older people go into the church hall.

Lloyd and Joe like going to church. 'They like seeing their friends. And the leaders are their friends, too. They have roles in the church, such as helping to get the room ready. They're part of the church stewarding team.'

'I learned and we learned together'

'The first year we were here, the Mothering Sunday service was an all-age, all-together family service. I was leading, and I thought it had gone really well. But then the notes flooded into the church letter-box. People didn't like the drama, they didn't like one of the songs we'd sung. I suspect that if we did the same service now, we wouldn't get the same reaction. But I was new and there was the element of uncertainty.

'I was a bit stunned. I'd no idea we would get that sort of reaction. I listened to the service again on tape to try to work out what it was that I'd done. But our senior minister was very supportive.

'I'd never had similar reactions in the six years before that, when I'd been doing schools work and had gone into churches as a visiting speaker. Gradually, it dawned on me that if you invite a visitor to your school, you *expect* things to be different. And, of course, if you don't like what he does, he isn't going to be there next week!

'It was a learning process. I learned and we learned together.'

'Don't be afraid of making mistakes'

'Recently, I came back after a fortnight's break and led a Sunday morning teaching session. After a holiday, you don't always feel highly motivated. But by the end of that Sunday morning I came away really excited, not because the teaching session had gone particularly well, but because I was surrounded by people, people I cared about, people who were my friends. I thought, *I belong here. We're different but we belong together.*

'All-age worship doesn't have to be child-centred. Don't feel you've got to engage everybody's attention all the time, I don't think you ever will. You need to be flexible. If what you're doing needs to grab the attention of seven-year-olds and it doesn't, move on. We always have a talk in our all-age services but I'm concerned if it lasts more than ten minutes. I'm not convinced people learn more if you preach longer. As Winston Churchill put it, "The mind cannot take in more than the seat can endure"!

'Don't be afraid of making mistakes, provided you learn from them. I certainly don't always get it right, though I think that after years of experience I recognise 90 percent of my own mistakes.'

'The climax of our worship'

'It's never been my ultimate goal that all ages should be together at all services every Sunday. There's scope for children and for teenagers in their own age-groups. But when children are there in the services, they should be helped to feel that this is where they belong.

'In a lot of churches, the children are in the service to begin with and then leave. We changed that five or six years ago, so that we're in our own teaching groups to begin with and then we come together as the climax of our worship. The last thing we experience on a Sunday morning is that we are God's family together.'

The congregation is scattered over a wide area, but the church has many geographically-based house-groups, which have a caring role. 'Caring goes on in all kinds of ways. The senior members, in particular, look after and visit each other and let the leadership know if anyone is in need. A lot of the older people in the church have been there all their lives and are related to one another. You'll discover that so-and-so is somebody's great-aunt.'

Hope for the future

'I hope our boys grow up to be happy and fulfilled, and have a strong Christian faith,' says Eunice. 'I hope there won't be any conflict between their faith and the way they have to live, and that they marry someone who shares their faith.'

Malc adds, 'We've always said that, whatever else happens, we hope the boys will always love Jesus. I also hope that when they grow up, we will still be friends. A year or so ago in a service, one of the other ministers was using balls of string to illustrate links of friendships. He chose

Lloyd and asked him, "Have you got a friend in the church?" Lloyd said, "Yes, my dad." I remember sitting there, feeling very proud and hoping that in ten years' time he would still feel the same.

'Our hopes for the church? That we'll go on working at being a family together, that we'll look outwards and live among the people around us as God's family. God has to give us the vision for that and the kind of compassion he has for the world.'

EVERYBODY PRAISE
all-age worship

A songbook which encourages churches to promote worship that is open to children and families. Mainly new material, in a variety of styles, but includes some songs that have not been easily available before. As well as the music edition, there is a words-only songbook plus a CD and an audio cassette.

'I think this *Everybody Praise* series should do what it was intended to do – unite people of all ages in praise to a living, loving God' (*Healing and wholeness* magazine, September 1997).

Music edition	ISBN 1 85999 172 6	£13.99
Words edition	ISBN 1 85999 178 5	£1.99
CD approx 50 mins	EAN 503359900 005 7	£12.99
Cassette approx 50 mins	EAN 503359900 004 0	£8.99

Available from your local Christian bookshop, or direct from Scripture Union on 01865 716880.

SCRAP HAPPY

A five-session resource for people of all ages, aimed at building cross-generational friendships.

The programme centres around brother and sister, Orlando and Kitty, and their encounter with the Scrap Family, a travelling group of actors who are performing a show called 'The Story of Luke'. Although on the surface the family seem fine, undercurrents of misunderstanding and unhappiness sour their relationships.

Through drama, games and activities, groups are encouraged to reflect on their experiences of family life and realise their value as individuals created by God. Photocopiable pages are included.

Designed to be used with *Scrap Happy: the Video* at all-age events, church weekends and holidays.

Book ISBN 1 85999 014 2 £7.99
Video ISBN 1 85999 046 0 £14.99

Available from your local Christian bookshop, or direct from Scripture Union on 01865 716880.